WHERE THERE'S A WILL ...

YOUR RIGHTS & OPTIONS

WHERE THERE'S A WILL …

A guide to setting up a Will and managing a loved one's estate

LIM FUNG PEEN

Marshall Cavendish Editions

© 2021 Marshall Cavendish International (Asia) Pte Ltd
Text © Lim Fung Peen

Published by Marshall Cavendish Editions
An imprint of Marshall Cavendish International

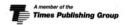
A member of the
Times Publishing Group

Other Marshall Cavendish Offices:
Marshall Cavendish Corporation, 800 Westchester Ave, Suite N-641, Rye Brook, NY 10573, USA • Marshall Cavendish International (Thailand) Co Ltd, 253 Asoke, 16th Floor, Sukhumvit 21 Road, Klongtoey Nua, Wattana, Bangkok 10110, Thailand • Marshall Cavendish (Malaysia) Sdn Bhd, Times Subang, Lot 46, Subang Hi-Tech Industrial Park, Batu Tiga, 40000 Shah Alam, Selangor Darul Ehsan, Malaysia

Marshall Cavendish is a registered trademark of Times Publishing Limited

National Library Board, Singapore Cataloguing-in-Publication Data

Name(s): Lim, Fung Peen.
Title: Where there's a will... : a guide to setting up a will and managing a loved one's estate / Lim Fung Peen.
Description: Singapore : Marshall Cavendish Editions, [2021]
Identifier(s): OCN 1252047113 | ISBN 978-981-4828-57-4 (paperback)
Subject(s): LCSH: Wills—Singapore--Popular works. | Estates (Law)—Singapore—Popular works.
Classification: DDC 346.5957054—dc23

Printed in Singapore

The statutes in the Annex are subject to copyright and are reproduced in this book with the permission of the Attorney-General's Chambers of Singapore. Readers may consult Singapore Statutes Online at https://sso.agc.gov.sg for the latest version of the statutes.

To Vanessa
We have had a wonderful life together
because He first loved us.
Thanks to Him and you.

In memory of Chyna,
Thank you for your love for 17 years,
especially through the pandemic.

CONTENTS

FOREWORD 9

PREFACE 11

ACKNOWLEDGEMENTS 15

GLOSSARY 17

1 INTRODUCTION 20

2 WHY IS A WILL IMPORTANT? 26

3 WHAT IS A WILL? 33

4 WHAT HAPPENS TO MY ASSETS WHEN I DIE? 48

5 INTESTACY (NON-MUSLIMS) – PASSING AWAY WITHOUT A WILL 66

6 COURT APPOINTMENT TO MANAGE AN ESTATE 77

7 EXECUTORS' DUTIES AND LIABILITIES 88

8 MUSLIM WILLS 105

9 ESTATE DUTY AND OTHER TAXES 115

10 FREQUENTLY ASKED QUESTIONS 121

CONCLUDING REMARKS 132

ANNEX   134

   Wills Act (Cap 352, 1996 Rev Ed)   136

   Intestate Succession Act (Cap 146,
   2013 Rev Ed)   150

   Inheritance (Family Provision) Act
   (Cap 138, 1985 Rev Ed)   154

   Probate and Administration Act
   (Cap 251, 2000 Rev Ed) – Extracts   160

   Legitimacy Act (Cap 162, 1985 Rev Ed)   184

ABOUT THE AUTHOR   191

FOREWORD

For some of us, death remains a subject that we would rather avoid discussing. We may believe that there is no hurry to consider the issue and that we have plenty of time left to do so. However, the general reluctance in our society to engage with end-of-life matters can unfortunately result in us delaying the issue until it is too late.

A Will is not merely a legal document. It is an expression of our wishes, and a way for us to continue providing for the needs of our loved ones even after we are gone. It is true that even without a Will, the default rules of intestate succession will apply to distribute our estate. However, these rules are blunt and inflexible, and may not take into account the specific needs and circumstances of our chosen beneficiaries. Our care and love for our families should not stop with death, and a Will is an easy way to ensure that they continue to be looked after when we are no longer around to do so.

Where there's a Will – A guide to setting up a Will and managing a loved one's estate is an essential read for everyone, regardless of their current stage of life. It provides solid practical guidance, whether one intends to make a Will or is preparing to fulfil the wishes of a loved one by assisting with the administration of an estate. Both perspectives are well covered in this book.

As with Fung Peen's first book, *Lasting Power of Attorney – A guide to the LPA and how to set it up*, *Where there's a Will* encourages us to consider end-of-life matters. The first book helps us to express our ideals and preferences in what may be our last years of life, while this book helps us and our loved ones to prepare for when we are gone. While the two books are natural complements to each other, they are complete pieces that may be read independently.

Once again, Fung Peen deftly cuts through the legal jargon to make potentially complex concepts understandable and accessible to everyone. He applies the same clear writing style that made his first book a pleasure to read, drawing upon practical examples from his numerous years of experience to illustrate his points. The addition of flowcharts in this book is a nice touch that helps the reader to easily visualise the concepts being discussed. As before, Fung Peen's genuine belief in his cause and his passion for helping others shines through the pages of this book; he has helped numerous people with their end-of-life matters and seen first-hand the impact of proper planning on their families.

As will be clear from this book, making a Will is neither a complex nor difficult exercise. Simply setting aside a little time to plan for the future can give us and our families considerable peace of mind. Fung Peen has once again done society a great service by making these important issues accessible to everyone.

Vincent Ooi
Lecturer of Law, Singapore Management University

PREFACE

In my other book, *Lasting Power of Attorney – A guide to the LPA and how to set it up*, I share the whys, whats and hows of setting up an LPA. This book is meant to be a companion volume as a Will and LPA should both be done, like having a pair of chopsticks or ear-phones! Having one just would not be complete or work as well.

For the last few years, when giving talks and webinars, I coined the phrase "A Will is a great way to love your family". This turn of phrase was inspired by my late father who had done his Will. He was taken from us too early, when I had just completed my stint in national service. I see my father's foresight in preparing his Will as an act of love that provided my family with some respite in our grief in settling his modest estate with minimal fuss and expense.

This book is written for you if you wish to consider finishing the journey of life well, so that there will be minimal fuss and complications for your family, friends and loved ones. Even though you are entitled to draft your own Will or do one online and there is no legal requirement to appoint a lawyer to do so, I would urge you to consult one no matter how simple you think your Will would be. Ultimately, your Will is a legal document and it is prudent to seek legal advice before finalising it.

Before I embarked on this book, my editor shared her observation with me:

> The average man on the street without a legal background appears to have very little or no knowledge about what to do or how to proceed when a loved one passes away. For example, most people would know whether their recently deceased parents have written a Will, but beyond that as to what action they should take on the passing of their parents, not many people seem to know how to proceed or the stages involved before assets and property can be properly dealt with. A focus on that track would be practical and useful, as opposed to information on how to draft a Will, which has been covered many times in various books.

Her observation rings with much truth and I could not have agreed more after being in legal practice for more than 25 years. During the COVID-19 global pandemic, the demand for drafting of Wills surged as a major concern for many people rose to the forefront – How do I ensure my children and elderly parents are taken care of if I am no longer around?

In such times, it is my hope that we will all learn from each other and be more aware, so that we are able to make better decisions about such matters.

I also observe that many expatriates who work here often have a much greater awareness of such matters and they do not assume that things would automatically be settled for them through some government scheme. Unfortunately, I have often heard Singaporeans with this rejoinder when asked if they have prepared their Will: "No need, lah, the Government will distribute my assets for me, right?"

It may be that expatriates often face tax issues in their home countries (for example, capital gains tax and inheritance tax) and this makes them more alert as to how they should manage their assets whilst they are alive and equally after they die, as they do not want to burden their estate or beneficiaries with tax payments. Though we may not have capital gains tax and inheritance tax in Singapore, we do have taxes known as Seller's Stamp Duty, Buyer's Stamp Duty and Additional Buyer's Stamp Duty that could be imposed on your beneficiaries without proper planning in the distribution of shares in your apartment or house. Having had the opportunity to practice in conveyancing and real estate law in Singapore, I have witnessed how some families ended up paying more in tax unwittingly because they did not consider this aspect and how their beneficiaries might end up paying such taxes.

My hope is that this book will not only benefit readers in Singapore but also those in common law countries with a tradition of making Wills, such as Malaysia, Australia, Hong Kong and beyond. If you decide to prepare your Will, I will, of course, recommend that you consult a lawyer in your own home country, or a lawyer in Singapore if you reside here.

The approach I aim to take in this book will be vastly different from my own experience as a law student, when I elected to pursue a year-long study in the law of succession and was introduced to the intricacies of the myriad statutes relating to succession law in the United Kingdom. That was no doubt an academic pursuit but this need not be one, as my editor rightly suggests. So lastly but certainly not the least, I pray that this book will also be useful to the next generation of legal practitioners, law students and young legal practitioners alike, who are looking to understand the practical aspects of succession law as they serve their clients in a wholistic manner and in their best interests.

I have used fictional stories as illustrations to make it easier to understand the practical consequences of making a Will. These stories are based on past cases and have been adapted and summarised to help the reader – all names, characters and events described in these stories are therefore fictitious.

ACKNOWLEDGEMENTS

Without the following people, this book would not have been possible.

Anita Teo, my editor, for taking another gamble on me and guiding me; Vincent Ooi for kindly agreeing to write the Foreword. To all my clients, both local and expatriates alike, who have worked with me to find practical solutions, especially in the recent pandemic and global lockdowns.

My wife and best friend, Vanessa, you are worth far more than a mountain of rubies (Proverbs 31:10-31); my pride and joy, Kimberley and Benjamin, for the laughter you fill our home with, and for not complaining when I work at home (Psalm 127:3) during the pandemic.

All at Yuen Law LLC, past and present, for joining me on this journey of learning and serving people. My team, Serene Tan, Brendan Kok and Kaysha Kuppusamy for helping me get through 2020 at work. Jolene Abelarde, my intern, for fine tuning research on privileged Wills and Anselm Chan for helping with the flowcharts. Lui Si Xuan, my practice trainee, for helping me to proofread.

To my first bosses, Tan Jing Poi and Daniel John, for being good role models, especially during the first decade of my career with the both of you. Your love for God, people and the law as well as your humility and integrity still inspire me today. Thank you for teaching me so many valuable things.

My cell group members from THCG and The Ark of CEFC, who have been a tremendous source of God's love, joy and assurance because of their constant focus on things eternal (Ephesians 1:11-14).

Last but in no way least, Jesus, my saviour, my strength and my all.

> A good person leaves an inheritance for their children's children, but a sinner's wealth is stored up for the righteous.
>
> **Proverbs 13:22**

Lim Fung Peen
LLB (Hons) London
Barrister-at-law (Middle Temple)
Advocate and Solicitor, Supreme Court of Singapore
Director, Yuen Law LLC

GLOSSARY

Adoption	A legally adopted child through an adoption order is deemed the lawful child of the adoptive parents. Such a person is entitled to a share under the laws of intestacy where there is no Will. This is not applicable under Muslim law, where an adopted child has no right to inheritance if the adoptive parents die and *vice versa*.
Administration of Estates	Process of collecting, transferring, liquidating and distributing a deceased's assets to the beneficiary(s).
Administrator	A person who is appointed by the court in a court order to manage the assets of a deceased person where there is no Will.
Beneficiary(ies)	The persons named in a Will or the next of kin entitled to benefit from a share in the distribution of the estate in accordance with the Intestate Succession Act (ISA) or the Administration of Muslim Law Act (AMLA).
Domicile	The country or state where a person is most closely connected to, and this is generally, but not always, where the individual has his permanent home. A person can possess only one domicile at any one time. Section 4 of the ISA provides that the distribution of the movable property of a deceased shall be governed by the law of the country in which he was domiciled at the time of his death; and the distribution of the immovable property of a deceased person shall be governed by the ISA wherever he may have been domiciled at the time of his death.
Estate	Assets and liabilities of a deceased at the time of his death.

Estate Duty	Tax imposed upon the value of a deceased's property.
Executor	Person appointed by a deceased in his Will to distribute his estate. The duties of an executor include collecting the assets, paying the lawful debts and taxes, and distributing the residue among the persons entitled. The executor must apply for and be appointed by a court order known as the "Grant of Probate" before he is authorised to carry out his duties.
Grant of Probate	A court order confirming that the Will is the last Will made by a deceased and appointing the executor(s) as the lawful authority to represent and deal with all matters relating to the estate.
Guardian	The exercise of parental responsibility over a child who is under 21 years of age. A legitimate child's parents are the natural guardians. An illegitimate child's mother is the natural guardian. Third parties can only be appointed under a Will or by a court order.
Issue	The issue of a person consists of his or her children (legitimate or legally adopted) and the descendants of any deceased children.
Joint Tenants	Ownership by two or more persons of the same property where there is the right of survivorship so that when one of the co-owners dies, the surviving joint owner inherits the deceased's property; upon the death of the other joint tenant, ownership will automatically pass on to the survivor(s). Property held as joint tenants does not form part of a person's estate and it cannot be disposed of by a Will or under the intestacy laws.
Grant of Letters of Administration	Court order appointing a person to legally administer the estate of a deceased where there is no Will.
Minor/Infant	A person under the age of 21 years old. An infant may be described as a minor. A minor has no full legal capacity. A minor cannot be an executor. The age of majority for a minor to claim a deceased member's nominated CPF monies is 18 years old.
Notary Public	A lawyer who is authorised to notarise documents by witnessing, authenticating and certifying the execution of documents to be used in foreign countries.

Presumption of Death	A person is assumed to be dead under the law when the person is absent for seven years.
Probate	The court process of proving that a Will is valid and appointing the executor to facilitate the administration of the estate of the deceased.
Resealing of Grant	Where the deceased's Grant of Probate is obtained in one of the Commonwealth countries, the grant must be re-sealed in the Singapore court so that the administrator/executor is appointed under a Singapore court order in order to be able to manage assets in Singapore.
Renounce	To give up the rights of inheritance or the right to apply for the Grant of Probate.
Tenants-in-Common	Where two co-owners own immovable property with distinct shares, for example a 50-50 share. The deceased's share of the property is distributed according to the terms of his Will. Where there is no Will, the deceased's share of the property will be distributed according to the intestacy laws, or the Muslim law. There is no right of survivorship for co-owners who own immovable property as tenants-in-common.
Testator/ Testatrix (f)	A person who makes a Will.
Trust	A legal arrangement where a person (trustee) holds property for the benefit of a beneficiary. The trust can be created during the lifetime of the settlor/donor or by a Will.
Trustee	A person appointed under the trust to hold and control the assets for the benefit of the true owner, known as the beneficiary.
Will	A legal document where a person appoints beneficiaries to receive assets upon the death of the maker of the Will and appoints a person (an executor) to manage the distribution of the assets to the beneficiaries.

1
INTRODUCTION

I started writing this book with much enthusiasm for researching the relevant varied and wide topics as I wanted this book to be as comprehensive as possible and, hopefully, be as useful to readers as possible. As I went deeper into the writing, I realised that I had not shared the guiding principles that I usually share with my own clients before they, too, dive into the numerous details of making decisions about the requirements for their own Wills. I do not want you to miss the forest for the trees. This often happens when we plunge straight into details without a suitable framework.

Just as we should warm up before embarking on physical exercises so as to prepare our bodies for exertion and avoid injury, I will take you through some basic "warm-ups" so that we avoid the common pitfalls of considering irrelevant matters or overthinking situations that we might foresee.

It best to start you off with some helpful considerations. So, let's warm up!

Don't Overthink

> If you have not completed your Will after a few months of starting on it, you might be overthinking.

By all means, you should think through your requirements carefully, but I would caution against overthinking. We are all prone to overthink matters sometimes due to our fear of missing out something important, wanting to be in full control of a situation or wanting to effect certain outcomes, even though we know that we cannot control the future and we cannot possibly provide for every scenario. In some extreme cases, overthinking will prevent a person from making decisions, due to a failure to accept the fact that a Will can never cover every possible situation, that one can always think of more issues to consider, and our life circumstances will continue to change. One indication of overthinking is not finalising and signing your Will after a few months of starting on it.

Simplicity is the ultimate sophistication.

– Leonardo Da Vinci

A healthier way to approach the making of a Will is to start with the basics in terms of distribution. Some common and basic distribution plans in Wills are as follows:

1. For a single person, distributing all of your assets to your immediate family or friends or charities in equal shares, and appointing one of the adult beneficiaries to be the sole executor.

2. If you are married without children, giving a share of all your assets to your spouse and your parent(s) or

charities, and appointing one of the adult beneficiaries to be the sole executor.

3. If you are married with children under 21, giving all of your assets to your spouse and if your spouse predeceases you, giving all of your assets to your child (or children equally). Both spouses should each do their Wills – this is commonly called mirror Wills. Here, you may consider appointing your spouse to be the executor and another adult, should your spouse predecease you, as a replacement executor.

Update, Update, Update

We are constantly encouraged to upgrade, re-train and stay relevant in order to stay employable or in business. This has become more pertinent following the COVID-19 pandemic. If you have a smart phone, you would be familiar with updating the operating system of your phone from time to time to ensure that it works optimally. It is the same situation with your Will, which should be updated from time to time as your life circumstances change, for example, the person you chose as an executor may no longer wish to be appointed for good reasons, the needs of your beneficiaries might have changed or your assets might have changed, too.

You should avoid the notion that your first Will is to be the only one you will ever have and it should last your entire lifetime. It would be most unfortunate if you have a Will which does not work well for your beneficiaries because it was not updated. It is not uncommon to encounter situations where, for example, an executor does not want to carry out his or her duties because of personal or health reasons, or the assets referred to in a Will no longer exists. This leaves the family or beneficiaries with challenges to overcome that often requires considerable time and legal fees to resolve.

Tips

Good occasions to update your Will:

1. When your children are grown up and their needs have changed.

2. When the executor of your Will is getting old, in declining health or facing changes in personal circumstances.

Get Organised

It is common for people to do their Wills without providing a list of assets to accompany the legal document. In the days of snail mail, this would not present much of a problem as financial institutions (banks, insurance companies, stock broking firms, etc), government statutory boards (HDB, CPF and IRAS) as well as major service providers (telcos, utilities companies, town councils, etc) all provided annual hard copy statements of accounts. However, we have been transitioning to receive such statements of accounts via email. Now, if your family members have no access to your email user ID and password, they will have no means of discovering what your assets are in order to collect and distribute them or how to settle your liabilities. This is a real challenge for many families when they find themselves unable to ascertain such important information.

List of assets

List all your assets by identifying them with the account number or address: bank account number, insurance policy number or full address of a property. It may be very useful to have the contact details of a person or organisation that can help with specific assets, for example, a bank representative, financial advisor, real estate agent, etc, so that your executor can seek their assistance if necessary. There is no need to list the value of the asset, as that is likely to change over time. The most crucial point is for your executor to be able to ascertain all of your assets and be able to settle your debts, too.

> Prepare a list of your assets and attach it to your Will.

If your executor is unable to ascertain all of your assets, they would have to engage the services of a lawyer to make formal inquiries on their behalf and this would add to the time and expense in processing the application for the court order known as the Grant of Probate.

Inform your executor

It may seem obvious that one should inform his or her intended executor that a Will is being drawn up but there are cases where an executor is not aware of having been appointed as one. Such situations can arise as the executor does not have to sign the Will and may not be present when one is made as there is no legal requirement for the executor to be present when a Will is signed. Only the maker of a Will (the testator/testatrix) and the witnesses need to sign the Will to fulfill the requirements under the Wills Act (WA).[1] This author has encountered cases where a named executor refused to carry out the role and renounced it in court, leaving the estate to find a replacement executor.

---

1 Wills Act (Cap 352, 1996 Rev Ed).

> Inform your executor where to locate your Will.

It is not only important for an executor to know that he or she is being appointed, but it is also imperative that the executor knows where to locate the Will, as well as how to determine the existence of the assets and liabilities of the estate. It would help the executor if the testator makes a list of assets and attaches it to the Will.

Funeral arrangements

Some individuals prefer to include instructions for their funeral arrangements in their Will. However, the usual practice is to open a Will only after the funeral and it would then be too late to read the instructions.

It should be noted that a Will is essentially a document to distribute one's assets and if you want to include such instructions and wishes in your Will, you should give specific instructions to your family and executor to read your Will before funeral arrangements are made.

Some may choose to attach a separate Statement of Wishes to specify their wishes for their funeral, such as cremation or burial, the type of religious rites, etc.

Whether included in a Will or a Statement of Wishes, it is merely a wish and therefore not legally binding.

> Share your funeral wishes with your family.

2

WHY IS A WILL IMPORTANT?

Reasons to Make a Will

One of the biggest disadvantages of not having a Will is that your family will be put to more inconvenience and have to bear an unnecessary burden if you do not put your affairs in order before you die. Most families struggle with the grief of losing a loved one and it is even more burdensome having to deal with cumbersome and time-consuming administrative processes if there is no Will.

One of the greatest advantages of having a Will is that it is the most efficient and cost-effective means to empower your personal representative to carry out your wishes. It is significantly more cumbersome, time-consuming and costly to manage a deceased's estate and affairs without a Will.

To be able to collect and distribute assets, the personal representative of the estate of the deceased needs to do the following:

1. obtain an authorisation from the court (under a court order known as a Grant); and
2. ascertain the lawful beneficiaries for distribution of the assets (under a Will or intestacy rules).

For a personal representative to be authorised by the court to carry out his or her duties to administer the estate, he or she needs to either:

1. apply for a Grant of Probate, where there is a Will appointing the personal representative to be the executor of the estate; or

2. apply for a Grant of Letters of Administration, in the absence of a Will.

With a Will, it is significantly quicker, more convenient and cheaper to obtain the Grant than without one. There are more legal requirements for obtaining a Grant of Letters of Administration when there is no Will compared to obtaining a Grant of Probate with a Will.

Obtaining a Grant of Probate with a Will

Obtaining a Grant of Letters of Administration without a Will.

Unfortunately, the primary concern of many people is the distribution of assets, that is, who gets what and how much. Some people are comfortable with the distribution plan dictated by the intestacy rules, where a spouse gets 50% of the assets and the children get the remaining 50%. If this is not the intention of the testator, then a Will should be done to avoid unintended consequences. Details of intestacy laws are set out in Chapter 5.

Many people are ignorant about the lesser-known but equally important aspect of managing a deceased person's assets, which is the legal process to appoint a personal representative for the estate of the deceased. The purpose of the legal process is for the personal representative to be authorised by the court (through a court order) to carry out the duties, such collecting and distributing the deceased's assets and paying outstanding debts. The personal representative is known as the *executor* where there is a Will and the court order is known as the Grant of Probate. The personal representative is known as the *administrator* where there is no Will and the court order is known as the Grant of Letters of Administration. Details of the legal process are set out in Chapter 6.

The top five reasons to do a Will are:

1. Appointing a trusted person to distribute your assets.
2. Choosing your beneficiaries and how much they should each inherit.
3. Saving significant expenses and time.
4. Ensuring a smoother administrative process.
5. Minimising family disputes.

The top three mistakes that people make are:

1. Assuming that their assets will be automatically distributed (by the Government).
2. Being ignorant of the process of settling their affairs after they die (such as applying to the court for a Grant).
3. Being ignorant of the negative consequences on their family if they do not have a Will.

Advantages of having a Will ☑	Disadvantages of not having a Will ☒
Choice of a responsible and able person whom you trust to manage your estate and distribute your assets	Dispute as to who should be appointed
Choice of beneficiaries who may not be able inherit your assets, especially those who are not primarily entitled under intestacy rules, such as parents, non-spouse, stepchildren	Beneficiaries are fixed by law
Choice of how much each beneficiary inherits	The share each beneficiary receives is fixed by law
Choice of guardians for children	Dispute as to who should be appointed
Appointment of trustees to care for beneficiaries under 21	Dispute as to who should be appointed

Examples of why a Will is important

A spinster's story

Madam Lee, an elderly spinster, died and left behind eight siblings. Her parents and two other siblings had died before her in 1950 and the 1960s. She was a co-owner of the family shophouse. She did not have a Will. Madam Lee's youngest sibling took up the role of settling her estate but ran into many challenges as she could not find the death certificates of her late parents and siblings, which made the application to court more complicated, resulting in a long-drawn and costly process. Under the intestacy rules, the late spinster's assets were also distributed to estranged siblings, which would not have been what Madam Lee intended.

If Madam Lee had made a Will, there would have been no requirement to produce the death certificates in court and thereby saving on time and legal expenses for her personal representative, not to mention also ensuring that her assets would be given only to her closer relatives.

A story of feuding grandparents

A young couple suffered a fatal car accident, leaving two young toddlers and the couple's respective parents. As the couple did not have Wills, 50% of his assets passed to his late wife and the other 50% to the two toddlers in equal shares. Both sets of grandparents ended up in court as both wanted to apply to the court to be the administrators of his estate and her estate. The application to obtain the Grant of Letters of Administration to appoint the administrators for his estate had to be completed before the application to obtain the Grant of Letters of Administration to appoint the administrators for her estate could start. Both sets of grandparents also went to court to apply to be the guardians of the two toddlers as neither of them could be automatically appointed the legal guardians.

With Wills, the process would have taken half the time and there would have been no dispute as to who would be the legal guardians of the children. Needless to say, the legal expenses would also have been minimised if the couple had made Wills.

A widow's story

Madam Tan and her late husband had talked about doing their Wills but always put it off due to their busy schedules. Her husband was estranged from his parents for 30 years as they had abandoned him. Madam Tan lost him suddenly to a heart attack. She was shocked to discover that his bank accounts were all frozen by the banks and she could not pay his credit card debts from his accounts when she informed the banks of his passing. She was aware that he had made investments and traded in shares. She started to worry as she was not sure what assets he had and how to pay his debts and loans.

Without a Will and with no children, his assets would be distributed 50% to his parents and 50% to his wife. This was never his intention as he wanted to benefit Madam Tan and the charities he supported. Madam Tan took almost a year to discover what his assets were, and this caused her application for the Grant of Letters of Administration to appoint herself the administrator for his estate to take much longer than usual. It was also very awkward for her to deal with her parents-in-law under the circumstances.

With a Will, his widow would not have been put to the cumbersome task of discovering his assets and the process to settle his estate would have taken a fraction of the time. Equally important, his intention of benefitting his wife and selected charities would have been clearly set out and he would have saved her the awkwardness of dealing with his estranged parents. Needless to say, she would also have saved on her legal expenses.

A story of remarriage

It was the second marriage for Rosa and Adrian. Each had an adult child from their first marriage. Rosa's son, Charles, grew very close to Adrian, and some said even closer than Adrian's own son, Marcus. Adrian wanted to adopt Charles but could not as Charles was already an adult. There was a bitter rivalry between Marcus and Charles. Adrian died without a Will, and without a Will, Charles was not entitled to inherit anything from Adrian's estate. As the lawful wife and son, Rosa and Marcus were each entitled to 50% of Adrian's estate. This further strained the family ties as Marcus refused to give Charles half of his share as requested by Rosa.

The simple option would have been for Adrian to do his Will to ensure that Charles inherited 25% of his estate, in the same way as if he had lawfully adopted Charles.

A PR's story

Candi was a Malaysian citizen and obtained Singapore Permanent Residence status as she had worked for many years in Singapore. Candi had bank accounts and owned property on both sides of the causeway. When she died, her husband Mike had to manage her assets in both countries. He started in Singapore as that was where he was based. He had to go to Malaysia to obtain her parents' death certificates as a required by the Singapore court to obtain the Grant of Letters of Administration. After that, he had to apply for a Resealed Grant of Letters of Administration in the Malaysian court before he could manage her assets in Malaysia.

With a Will, Mike would have been able to process the Grant of Probate in Singapore and subsequently the Resealed Grant in Malaysia significantly faster and with less expense. He would not have needed to trouble himself with obtaining the death certificates of her parents as well.

Karen's story – the plight of being illegitimate

Karen's parents never married. Her mother had left her and she was raised by her father, Mark, singlehandedly. Mark was too busy to go through the process of legally adopting her. Fortunately, Mark learned that since Karen was an illegitimate child in the eyes of the law and he had not adopted her, she would not inherit anything from him! He immediately made a Will and made her a beneficiary.

When Karen became an adult, she learnt that due to her illegitimate status, her assets would have gone to her mother and not Mark under the law! Karen immediately did her Will to make sure that Mark would inherit her assets and not her mother.

3

WHAT IS A WILL?

Before 1600s, the UK had various customary rules for the giving of personal property by Will. The power to gift real property by Will was granted by the Statute of Wills 1540. Formal steps were then prescribed under the Statute of Frauds 1677 for the creation of a valid Will, including the requirement that a Will of real property must be in writing. In 1837, the UK enacted the Wills Act.[1] The UK Wills Act 1837 formed the basis of the 1838 Indian Wills Act.[2] By 1830, Singapore was grouped together with Penang and Malacca to form the Straits Settlements, which was administered by the British East India Company. The Indian Wills Act was in turn adopted by Singapore in 1838. Since then, there have been several amendments.

How to Make a Valid Will

To make a valid Will, the following must be complied with under sections 4, 5 and 6 of the Wills Act (WA):[3]

1. It must be in writing.
2. The maker of a Will must be at least 21 years old.
3. The maker must sign the Will at the foot of the Will.
4. The maker's signature must be witnessed by two or more witnesses, who must also sign the Will in his or her presence.

---

1 Wills Act 1837 (c 26) (UK).
2 Wills Act 1838 (Act No XXV of 1838) (India).
3 Wills Act (Cap 352, 1996 Rev Ed).

5. The witnesses cannot be beneficiaries of the Will, or
   spouses of beneficiaries.

By the Wills (Amendment) Act 1992,[4] changes were made to
enable a Will to be valid under Singapore law if it complies with
the formal requirements of another legal system. This applies
to the Will of any testator who dies after that time, regardless
of the date of execution of the Will – it does not apply to
testators who died before the commencement of the 1992 Act.
This is a welcomed provision as there are more expatriates and
foreigners owning assets in Singapore and there is a need to
administer part of their estate here. One procedural benefit is
the dispensation of the need to apply complicated common law
conflicts of law principles which used to be applicable. Under
the current section 5 of the WA, a Will is deemed as validly
executed if its execution conformed to the internal law in force
in the territory where it was executed, or in the territory where,
at the time of its execution or at the time of the testator's death,
he was domiciled or had his habitual residence, or in a state
of which, at either of those times, he was a national. A Will
which disposes immovable property is also treated as properly
executed if its execution conformed to the internal law in force
in the territory where the property was situated.

Beneficiaries should not be witnesses

Section 10 of the WA provides that where a witness or the
spouse of a witness receives a gift under the Will, the gift will
be void. In all other respects, however, the Will remains valid.
Where Wills are professionally drafted, this provision is unlikely
to present any problem.

---

4 Wills (Amendment) Act 1992 (No 24 of 1992).

As this rule is not commonly known, it is by no means uncommon for gifts to fail on this ground where a testator writes his own Will without any legal assistance. Such a problem usually arises in situations such as a DIY Will which is done urgently without the assistance of a lawyer.

In the English case of *In the Estate of Bravda*,[5] the testator made a home-made Will in which he left his entire estate to his two daughters from his first marriage. He was estranged from his second wife. He had four witnesses to his Will, namely, his daughters and two others, who were not beneficiaries. The Court of Appeal held that as the daughters were witnesses to the Will, they could not benefit under it, given the clear language of the English equivalent of section 10. The estate therefore passed in its entirety to the testator's second wife, an outcome which he had clearly sought to avoid. The result of the case was certainly most unfortunate, and all the judges of the Court of Appeal expressed their regret at what they felt the statute forced them to decide. Two of them called for the Wills Act 1837 to be amended so that, where there are two independent credible witnesses, the mere fact that a beneficiary has also signed as a witness should not operate to defeat the intention of the testator. A short amending statute – the Wills Act 1968 – was passed in the same year that the case was decided by the Court of Appeal.

Section 10(2) of the WA now helps to avoid that unfortunate situation. This subsection applies to the Will of any person dying after the passing of the 1992 Act, regardless of the date of execution of the Will.

---

5   *In the Estate of Bravda* [1968] 1 WLR 479.

Must be written – no verbal Wills

In 2010, the High Court decided that a verbal Will was not valid.[6]

Madam Tan Kiok Lan had five children and she made a verbal Will on 16 July 2009. Her verbal instructions were given to an employee of a Will writing company. A draft Will was prepared based on Madam Tan's verbal instructions but, unfortunately, she passed away on 30 July 2009 without signing the Will.

A declaration was sought that the Madam Lee's verbal instructions amounted to a nuncupative Will (verbal Will), amounting to her valid last Will and testament and that the draft Will comprised the details of that verbal Will. The court held that the formalities required of a valid Will were clearly set out in the WA. If those formalities were not met, and unless the testator fell within a statutory exception, the Will would not be valid. A nuncupative Will is, therefore, not valid unless it is made by a person falling within section 27 of the WA.[7]

Will revoked upon marriage

Section 13 of the WA provides for a Will to be revoked automatically when the testator marries. The proviso to this section provides for an exception where a Will is expressed to be made in contemplation of a marriage and the marriage contemplated is solemnised. Although the WA makes provision for marriage, it ignores the possibility of divorce. Divorce does not revoke a Will (the new English legislation provides that a gift to a former spouse contained in a Will lapses on dissolution of the marriage, except in so far as a contrary intention appears

---

6   *Tan Pwee Eng v Tan Pwee Hwa* [2010] SGHC 258.

7   In *pari materia*, Wills Act 1837 (c 26) (UK) s 11 read with Wills (Soldiers and Sailors) Act 1918 (c 58) (UK) s 1.

in the Will). Of course, a client who is contemplating divorce proceedings should be advised to consider changing his or her Will. With the rising number of divorces in Singapore, it may be worthwhile for the Singapore Parliament to consider adopting the English position, too.

Common Types of Wills

Each person must do their own Will. It is one Will per person. However, it is common for couples to do each of their own Wills but with similar content and intention. These are known as mirror Wills and mutual Wills. There is one major difference between these two types of Wills.

Mirror Will

A mirror Will is made by two people, often with similar terms in two separate Wills. Married couples often do mirror Wills as their intentions and outcomes are usually very similar, if not identical. A typical mirror Will would have similar provisions to its counterpart and could work like this:

1. One spouse gives all assets to the surviving spouse, with the surviving spouse as the executor.
2. If both pass on, then all assets are given to the other beneficiaries (such as children, parents, siblings, charities, etc).

Commons clauses would also include those relating to replacement executors or appointment of guardians.

Mirror Wills are different from mutual Wills in that there is no agreement between the parties not to change their Wills. Parties making mirror Wills must fully accept the right of the survivor to change his or her Will as and when they see fit.

Mutual Will

Mutual Wills can be made by two people pursuant to a separate agreement between them to make the Wills and not revoke them without the consent of the other. Each party would have a separate Will making provisions for the other party on substantially similar terms, dealing with the same property. Parties will also have a binding contract between them, which will typically provide that:

1. Each of the parties will leave their property to mutually agreed beneficiaries.
2. Neither party will revoke or make any changes to his or her Will without the consent of the other during their joint lifetimes.
3. Upon the death of one party, the survivor will not revoke the Will or alter it so as to change the mutually agreed beneficiaries.

The agreement can be made orally or in writing on a separate document. It is advisable for parties to set out the agreement on a separate document and have the terms reflected in the Wills to avoid future problems of proving the agreement.

It is also advisable for parties to make it clear in writing that the Wills are mutual Wills to ensure that the beneficiaries, upon the death of the first party, are aware that they are benefiting under a mutual Will. This would allow beneficiaries to know their position in case the surviving spouse makes a new Will with no reference to the mutual Will.

Mirror Wills v Mutual Wills

Mirror will	Mutual Will
Flexibility in providing for change in circumstances	Surviving spouse is prevented from altering the Will
Does not require any consent and is not bound by any agreement to not alter the Will	Alterations require consent and parties are bound by a written agreement to not alter the Will
Requires at least two legal documents	Requires at least three legal documents
More flexible	More costly

Identify Beneficiaries Clearly

In the case of *Re Will of Samuel Emily*,[8] the High Court was asked by the executrix to interpret the Will as it lacked clarity as regards the beneficiaries. The testatrix was a spinster and her estate was worth $1.7 million. In her Will, she made gifts to various charities and $250,000 to the Lam family. The executrix was a close family friend and the executrix's husband had drafted the Will. The court in that case commented:[9]

> It can be seen, without any disrespect to the drafter, that the will was prepared in a rather casual fashion. In fact, p 3 of the will is in a different font from the rest of the five-page will (including the backing sheet). There was obviously no great effort made to ascertain the proper descriptions and addresses of the various intended beneficiaries. ...

> Such casualness is understandable considering the very close and warm relationship that the testatrix had with the executrix and presumably with her late husband as well. It was not so much a case of solicitor meeting client as a situation of

8 *Re Will of Samuel Emily* [2001] SGHC 299.
9 *Re Will of Samuel Emily* [2001] SGHC 299 at [31]–[32].

family friends meeting to discuss the testatrix's future wishes. Obviously, they understood one another so well that it never occurred to them that an outsider reading the will would not know immediately what some terms like "the Lam family" signify.

As this case illustrates, care should be taken in drafting a Will. There should be as much clarity as possible to minimise the need for court intervention. It is sometimes not possible to gather the precise name or ID number of a beneficiary, but all reasonable steps should be taken to ascertain the identity of the person or charity, as the case may be. We may not know the full names of persons or we commonly refer to charities by their common names, but these are often not their legal names. In Samuel Emily's case, she referred to Cancer Society instead of Singapore Cancer Society, Spastic Society of Singapore instead of Spastic Children's Association of Singapore, Dr Chen Su Lan's Home instead of the Chen Su Lan Methodist Children's Home, Kidney Foundation instead of National Kidney Foundation, The Salvation Home instead of The Salvation Army and St Luke's Hospital instead of St Luke's Hospital for the Elderly Ltd.

Privileged Wills of NSFs and NSmen[10]

It has been long thought since Roman times that privileged Wills with less stringent requirements are necessary because of a soldier's lack of access to legal advice and being faced with imminent mortal danger.

---

10 NSFs are full-time National Servicemen serving the two-year mandatory National Service (NS), while NSmen have completed the mandatory NS and have transitioned to being operationally ready reservists.

Section 27 of the WA allows a narrow group of individuals to make a privileged Will. While no cases have been adjudicated in Singapore, section 11 of the UK Wills Act 1837 read with section 1 of the Wills (Soldiers and Sailors) Act 1918[11] is in *pari materia*, and the law in Singapore will likely develop similarly.

Privileged Wills were practically necessitated by mortal danger[12] and a lack of access to legal advice,[13] especially at sea where it may be a long time before one can have access to lawyers to abide by formalities. Especially with respect to a conscript army like Singapore's, it can be seen as a way to recognise the special role of a drafted soldier.[14]

From before the 1990s, Singapore Armed Forces (SAF) personnel have had involvement in the United Nations (UN) Transition Assistance Group (UNTAG) during Nambia's elections, UN peacekeeping mission to restore peace and security in Timor-Leste, International Security Assistance Force (ISAF) peace support operations and reconstruction efforts in Afghanistan led by the North Atlantic Treaty Organization (NATO), UN Transitional Authority in Cambodia (UNTAC), UN mission overseeing the electoral process in Cambodia and counter-piracy effort in the Gulf of Aden.

Though it may appear that soldiers carrying out peacekeeping duties would not qualify, I respectfully agree with Denning

---

11 Wills (Soldiers and Sailors) Act 1918(c 58) (UK) ss 1–3 & 5(2).
12 *Drummond v Parish* (1843) 3 Curt 522.
13 Jack Tsen-Ta Lee, "A Place for the Privileged Will" (1994) 15 *Singapore Law Review* 176.
14 J Rudnicki, "The axiology of military wills" (2015) 2(1) *European Journal of Comparative Law and Governance* 16.

LJ when he opined in *Re Wingham, Andrews v Wingham* (*Wingham*)[15] that:

> Doubtful cases may arise in peacetime when a soldier is in, or is about to be sent to, a disturbed area or an isolated post, where he may be involved in military operations. As to these cases, all I can say is that, in case of doubt, the serving soldier should be given the benefit of the privilege.

Many SAF duties concern peace time training and humanitarian operations, as well as routine unit duty overseas which are unlikely to be considered "active military service" as there is no threat of war or imminent war.

NSFs are posted into three different services: the SAF, the Singapore Civil Defence Forces (SCDF) and the Singapore Police Force (SPF). Within the SAF, NSFs can be posted into three different arms, namely, the Army, the Air Force and the Navy. The privilege provided by section 27 of the WA applies in two "narrow"[16] circumstances. First, for "soldiers" in "actual military service" and second, for "mariner or seaman" "at sea".[17] In such situations, these individuals will be given the benefit of making a valid Will without needing to observe the formalities required. The only requirement is that the words must be spoken with the intention that they have testamentary effect.[18] Therefore, words spoken in casual conversations are insufficient.[19] Gifts to

---

15 *Re Wingham, Andrews v Wingham* [1949] P 187 at 196.

16 *Tan Pwee Eng v Tan Pwee Hwa* [2011] 1 SLR 113 at [12].

17 See actual wording of s 27(1): "Notwithstanding anything in this Act, any soldier being in actual military service, or any mariner or seaman being at sea, may dispose of his personal estate as he might have done before the making of this Act and may do so even though under the age of 21 years."

18 Andrew G Lang, "Privileged will – a dangerous anachronism?" (1985) 8 Univ of Tas LR 167.

19 *Re Knibbs, Flay v Trueman* [1962] 2 All ER 829, [1962] 1 WLR 852.

witnesses of privileged Wills are also not void since no attestation by witnesses is necessary in the first place.[20]

"Soldier" in "active military service"
"Soldier"

Pursuant to the Singapore Armed Forces Act,[21] a "soldier" means any person who is a member of the SAF and includes a servicewoman. In common law, this includes persons undergoing military training.[22] Therefore, this interpretation may be extended to section 27 of the WA and NSFs are likely considered "soldiers" within the meaning of section 27.

Significantly, *Wingham* held that soldiers also include those outside of the "force".[23] In particular, these include members of forces who work both at their jobs and man defences. This would mean that those posted to the SCDF and SPF may, under common law, fall under the meaning of soldier in section 27.

Although most NSFs are under 21 years of age, section 27 expressly provides that privileged Wills are available to those under 21 years old.

"In active military service"

However, NSFs are unlikely to be considered "in active military service". As espoused by Denning LJ in *Wingham*, active military service is "service that is directly concerned with operations in a war which is or has been in progress or is imminent".[24] In particular, Denning LJ opined that soldiers serving at home or

---

20 *Re Limond, Limond v Cunliffe* [1915] 2 Ch 240.
21 Singapore Armed Forces Act (Cap 295, 2000 Rev Ed) s 2(1).
22 *Re Stanley* [1916] P 192.
23 *Re Donaldson* (1840) 2 Curt 386.
24 *Re Wingham, Andrews v Wingham* [1949] P 187 at 196.

on routine duty overseas (the local equivalent being overseas joint exercises) in times of peace cannot use the privilege.[25] This is consistent with section 2(3) of the Singapore Armed Forces Act, which defines "active service" as a person "engaged in operations against the enemy" or in a place "occupied by an enemy".

NSFs can make a valid privileged Will if Singapore or the world is at war or if war is "imminent". In *Wingham*, a soldier was on operational duty as a trainee pilot in Canada during World War II. Saskatchewan was only a day's flight from the enemy. Bucknill LJ and Cohen LJ felt that since the deceased testator was liable at any time to be ordered to proceed to some area to take part in an ongoing war,[26] he was in "actual military service". This is consistent with Denning LJ's opinion that being liable to be mobilised to an imminent war would provide the benefit of the privilege. In a situation of war where Singapore is or may become involved in, NSFs and all other operationally ready servicemen are likely to be given the benefit to make a privileged Will under section.[27]

Those posted to the SCDF and SPF are unlikely to be considered as being in "active military service" despite the fact that their postings may entail greater imminent danger in peace time. However, those deployed to postings against terrorists or insurgences may fall under the meaning of active military service.

Since the privilege is limited to war or "war-like"[28] situations, soldiers or civilians on humanitarian missions may not be given the privilege under section 27 even thought they might

25 *Re Wingham, Andrews v Wingham* [1949] P 187 at 196.
26 *Re Wingham, Andrews v Wingham* [1949] P 187 at 196.
27 *Re Jones* [1981] Fam 7, [1981] 1 All ER 1.
28 *Re Wingham, Andrews v Wingham* [1949] P 187 at 197.

not have access to legal advice. For instance, this would not include the volunteers and soldiers deployed to Indonesia and Thailand to provide assistance during the 2004 tsunami,[29] even though it posed a continued risk. This may overly limit the purpose of section 27 in providing succession planning for circumstanced individuals.

Seamen and mariners "at sea"

The requirements for those "at sea" is arguably more relaxed. For the privilege to apply, it is not necessary that the Will is executed at sea, so long as it is made while on maritime service.[30] This privilege has applied even if the ship is stationed in the harbour[31] or the individual is on shore leave. The nature of the service is immaterial.[32] This suggests that any NSF who is posted to a ship, likely those posted to the Navy, can make a privileged Will even if there is no connection to war or any "war-like" operation.

However, those doing their reservist training who may be posted to a ship are unlikely to be given this privilege since these are short-term postings.[33]

Army Deployment Force

As an erstwhile point, those part of the Army Deployment Force[34] on peacekeeping missions are likely to be given the benefit of the privilege since it may be considered a "disturbed area" even in peace time. In *Re Jones*, the English court found

---

29 Overseas operations <https://www.mindef.gov.sg/web/portal/mindef/defence-matters/exercises-and-operations/exercises-and-operations-detail/overseas-operations> (accessed 14 December 2020).
30 *Re Rapley's Estate, Rapley v Rapley* [1983] 3 All ER 248 at 251, [1983] 1 WLR 1069 at 1073.
31 *Re M'Murdo* (1868) LR 1 P & D 540.
32 *Re Rapley's Estate, Rapley v Rapley* [1983] 3 All ER 248 at 251, [1983] 1 WLR 1069 at 1073.
33 *Barnard v Birch* [1919] 2 IR 404.
34 Army Deployment Force <https://www.mindef.gov.sg/oms/arc/our-careers-army-deployment-force.html> (accessed 14 December 2020).

that there was active military service while patrolling because of the circumstances of Northern Ireland in the 1980s. This may be similar to peacekeeping missions like those to assist UNTAG during Nambia's elections, participating in the NATO-led ISAF peace support operations and reconstruction efforts in Afghanistan and even the counter-piracy effort in the Gulf of Aden.[35]

Revoking a privileged Will

It should be noted that returning to life as a civilian does not in and of itself operate as revocation.[36] Therefore, individuals should be advised to create a formal Will or revoke the privileged Will after operations or leaving the Navy.

Making Wills in Other Jurisdictions

If you are making a Will in a Commonwealth country (for example, Malaysia, Brunei, Australia, New Zealand, India, the UK), the formal requirements are very similar to the requirements in Singapore.

In European countries such as Germany, France, Italy and Spain, Wills are commonly made in the presence of notaries and they are referred to as notarised or public Wills. Holographic or private Wills can also be done but this is not as common. China has similar rules: a notarial Will is one made by a testator through a notary agency, and a testator-written Will is one made in the testator's own handwriting, signed by him and witnessed by two or more witnesses.[37]

---

35 Overseas operations <https://www.mindef.gov.sg/web/portal/mindef/defence-matters/exercises-and-operations/exercises-and-operations-detail/overseas-operations> (accessed 14 December 2020).

36 *Re Booth, Booth v Booth* [1926] P 118 at 135.

37 Law of Succession of The People's Republic of China (Order No 24 of the President of the People's Republic of China, effective as of 1 October 1985) Art 17.

It is best to seek legal and tax advice on whether you should do separate Wills for different jurisdictions or have one Will to dispose of all your assets in various jurisdictions.

4

WHAT HAPPENS TO MY ASSETS WHEN I DIE?

For a better understanding of why it is beneficial to make a Will, it is useful to consider this question – What happens to my assets when I die?

As there are many types of assets, only the most common assets such as HDB flats, private property, bank accounts, public listed shares, private limited shares and insurance payouts will be addressed.

Immovable Property

Immovable properties (such as HDB flats, condominiums, landed, industrial or commercial) are commonly purchased by married couples as co-owners. Other co-owners include parent and child, and siblings. Many of these co-owners assume that when one co-owner dies, the survivor becomes the sole owner, and they would be correct if the manner of holding the immovable property is as joint tenants. But it not uncommon for some owners to co-own as tenants-in-common, too – this is usually when people come together to invest in property and want to spell out clearly their shares based on their contributions.

Two brothers and a HDB flat

John and Charles bought a HDB flat as joint tenants. When John married Mary, she lived with John at the HDB flat. Mary and Charles did not get along. John was a simple man and only owned the HDB flat and had two bank accounts, one of which was jointly held with his brother. John passed on after a serious illness without children, and without making a Will. Charles became the sole owner of the HDB flat and he asked Mary to move out as he needed to rent out the rooms for income.

For Mary to inherit John's share of the HDB flat, John should have severed the joint tenancy so that he was the 50% owner and made a Will to give Mary his share.

When Harry left Sally

Harry and Sally were unhappily married for many years with one daughter. Harry was very filial son, but his parents never approved of Sally. Both Harry and Sally had amassed substantial wealth from the few condominiums they co-owned as tenants-in-common in equal shares. Harry left Sally and eventually asked her for a divorce. Sally agreed to a divorce. Harry told his mother that he wanted to leave most of his wealth to his daughter and some to his parents and hoped that they would help to care for his daughter if something should happen to him. Before Harry and Sally started on the divorce proceedings, Harry died from a massive brain aneurysm. As he was still legally married to Sally, she was entitled to apply for the Grant of Letters of Administration, and she was entitled to 50% of his assets and their daughter the other 50%.

Harry's parents were livid as they wanted to take charge of his affairs and fight for a bigger share of his assets for their granddaughter and a small share for themselves to honour what Harry had said to them. They were rightly advised that they had no right to do so under the intestacy rules. Harry's 50% share as a tenant-in-common in all the condominiums he owned with Sally would be distributed equally to Sally and their daughter. As parents, they were not entitled to anything under the intestacy rules.

With a troubled marriage, Harry should have made a Will to ensure that his wishes were legally enforceable by his parents.

HDB Flat Inheritance
Ownership eligibility applicable to Singapore Citizens
and Permanent Residents only

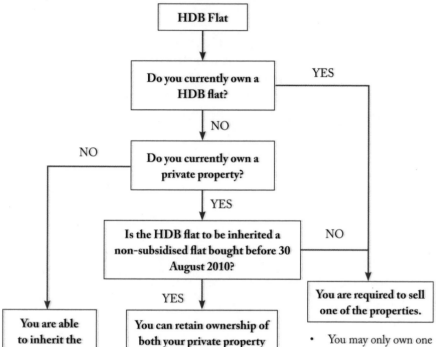

*To retain ownership of the HDB flat, you must meet prevailing ownership eligibility conditions (family nucleus and citizenship) and you and your family must live in the HDB flat.

- You may only own one HDB flat at any one point in time.
- If you decide to sell your private property and retain the HDB flat, you must still fulfil HDB's prevailing ownership eligibility conditions before disposing of your private property.

Inheriting Private Property

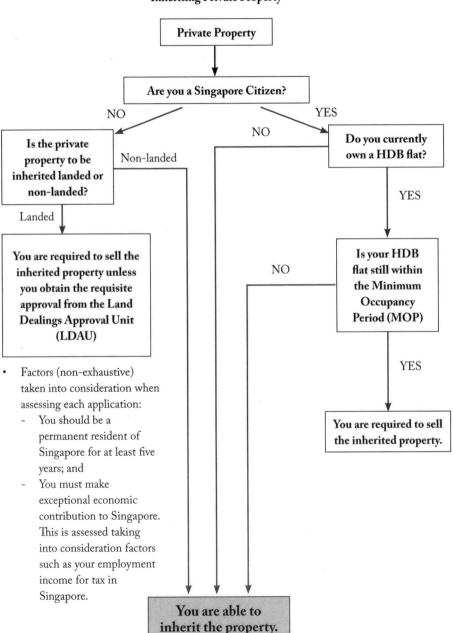

```
                    ┌─────────────────────┐
                    │   Private Property  │
                    └─────────────────────┘
                               │
                               ▼
                 ┌──────────────────────────────┐
                 │  Are you a Singapore Citizen? │
                 └──────────────────────────────┘
        NO                                      YES
```

Is the private property to be inherited landed or non-landed?

Non-landed

Do you currently own a HDB flat?

NO

YES

Landed

You are required to sell the inherited property unless you obtain the requisite approval from the Land Dealings Approval Unit (LDAU)

Is your HDB flat still within the Minimum Occupancy Period (MOP)

NO

- Factors (non-exhaustive) taken into consideration when assessing each application:
  - You should be a permanent resident of Singapore for at least five years; and
  - You must make exceptional economic contribution to Singapore. This is assessed taking into consideration factors such as your employment income for tax in Singapore.

YES

You are required to sell the inherited property.

You are able to inherit the property.

Joint tenancy v Tenancy-in-common

Joint tenancy

Conceptually, joint tenancy is a situation where two people own 100% of the flat or house with no distinct shares for each owner. Joint tenancy is an operation of property law (as opposed to a joint bank account which is fundamentally a contractual relationship between a customer and the bank on how the account is to be operated by the customer).

Joint Tenancy

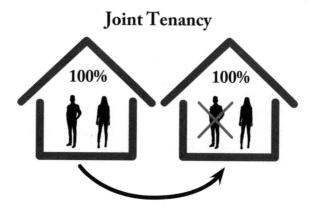

This means that upon the death of one of the joint tenants, the deceased joint tenant ceases to have a share in the flat or house. The effect is that the remaining joint tenant's share has been enlarged by acquiring the deceased's share. Any provision in a Will does not affect a property held as joint tenants.

In joint tenancy, the right of survivorship applies. This means that upon the demise of any joint owner, his interest in the flat would automatically be passed on to the remaining co-owner(s). This is regardless of whether the deceased joint owner has left behind a Will.

> **Examples of joint tenancy**
>
> Mr and Mrs A own a HDB flat under joint tenancy. In the event of Mr A's demise, the ownership of the flat will automatically be passed to Mrs A.
>
> Mr A, Mr S (son) and Ms D (daughter) own a landed property under joint tenancy. In the event of Mr A's demise, the ownership of the landed property will automatically be passed to Mr S and Ms D. Mr S and Ms D will be co-owners as joint tenants, unless they apply to sever their joint tenancy to become tenants-in-common.

The automatic transfer of ownership in the property stops at the surviving joint tenant. The surviving joint tenant should do a Will to ensure that the property then goes to the desired beneficiaries when he or she passes on.

> Joint tenants should do a Will so that when they become the sole owner (through the rights of survivorship), they are clear about who the property should pass to on their demise.

Tenancy-in-common

Tenancy-in-Common

X% | Y%

No rights of survivorship

Under tenancy-in-common, each co-owner holds a separate and distinct share in the property.

The right of survivorship does not apply. Upon the demise of a co-owner, the deceased's interest in the property will be distributed according to his or her Will, if any. If there is no Will, his or her interest in the property will be distributed in accordance with the provisions of the Intestate Succession Act (ISA).[1]

> ### Examples of tenancy-in-common
>
> Two brothers, Mr A and Mr B, own a HDB flat under tenancy-in-common with 50% and 50% shares, respectively. In the event of Mr A's demise, his ownership in the flat (his 50% share) will be distributed according to his Will, or according to the provisions of the ISA. His brother, Mr B, does not automatically own his brother's 50% share.
>
> Ben and Jerry buy a commercial shophouse as an investment, with a contribution of 80-20 towards the purchase price. To protect his interest, Ben would want to hold the property as tenants-in-common with 80% in his name so that he can write a Will to give his 80% share to his beneficiaries and Jerry can do the same with his 20% share.

> Tenants-in-common should do a Will to ensure that each of their share in the property goes to the desired beneficiaries.

Bank Accounts

When a bank is notified of the death of an account holder, it will immediate "freeze" all of the deceased person's bank accounts, be it a sole bank account or a jointly-held one. This usually applies to all accounts, regardless of whether they are savings, current, fixed deposits or investment accounts. In practice, the bank puts in place a "hold code" and "tags" the affected account as "holder

---

1 Intestate Succession Act (Cap 146, 2013 Rev Ed).

deceased" to indicate the status of the account. This also applies to joint accounts.

A story of secret joint bank accounts

Roger and Jessica were happily married with children. They did not have a joint account with each other, but little did they know that Jessica had a joint account with her single sister and Roger with his single brother. They only found out when their lawyer asked them about bank accounts when preparing their Wills. They were slightly embarrassed but relieved when they discovered that the funds in these joint accounts belonged entirely to their single siblings and their names had only been added merely for convenience. With this newfound knowledge, they included a clause in each of their own Wills to give the funds in the joint accounts to their respective siblings, and they reminded their own siblings to do their own Wills to make sure that the funds would go to their desired beneficiaries as well.

With their Wills, Roger and Jessica managed to avert a potential dispute in the event that their children should decide to challenge their aunt and uncle for the funds on the basis that their parents were joint account holders.

Jake's story of closing Amy's bank accounts

Jake and Amy were married for 45 years. When Amy passed away, Jake went to the bank to close her two bank accounts, one in her sole name and one in their joint names. He showed the bank officer their marriage certificate and her death certificate. The bank officer told Jake that he could not close the accounts and withdraw the funds with only those documents. Jake was surprised and insisted that it was what Amy would have wanted. The officer explained that the bank needed a Grant of Probate or Grant of Letters of Administration authorising Jake to do so and apologised for the inconvenience. Jake asked to close at least the joint account since he was the joint account holder, but the officer said that the terms of the joint account did not permit him to do so.

> If Amy had done a Will, the time and legal expenses involved in obtaining the Grant of Probate would be significantly less than obtaining the Grant of Letters of Administration if she did not have a Will.

Why do banks freeze accounts?

When a bank account is opened, the account holder agrees to the bank's terms and conditions, and banks commonly have the right to suspend or close accounts. This gives the bank the right to freeze a bank account. Why do banks do this? Well, banks have this prudent practice as a safeguard to minimise the risk of unauthorised withdrawals. No bank would want to pay out sums of money to a person not entitled to the money. Furthermore, banks are not in a position to verify who is entitled and who is not. To avoid this risk, banks will only pay out to the person(s) lawfully authorised and named in a court order. This court order is known as a Grant of Probate, where a deceased has made a Will, or a Grant of Letters of Administration, where there is no Will.

> Where there's a Will, the process to obtain the Grant of Probate is faster and cheaper than obtaining the Grant of Letters of Administration where there's no Will.

Joint bank accounts

> **Myth v Fact**
>
> *Myth*: Surviving joint account holders have the right to close the accounts and take over the funds. *Fact*: Unless there is a right of survivorship clause as part of the terms and conditions for the bank account, the surviving joint bank account holder does not have the right to the money.

In most situations, being a joint account holder only provides the account holder with the authority to withdraw the funds in pre-agreed modes (from ATMs, via cheques, etc). Most joint accounts operate like a lock with two keys: some are joint and require both keys before money can be withdrawn (for example, two signatories), while others are joint/alternate and any one key can unlock the funds; but in both cases, when one key is missing (if one of the bank account holder dies), the lock is frozen for safety reasons.

If there is no right of survivorship for a joint bank account, banks may sometimes exercise their discretion and allow the surviving joint account holder to close the account and take the funds. This is usually the case where the amount of the funds is not large or if there are exceptional circumstances. Banks sometimes also exercise their discretion and allow a family member to close the account and take the funds but, again, usually only where the amount of the funds is not large or if there are exceptional circumstances. Some local banks are quite strict about this and do not have a threshold amount, and will insist on having sight of the Grant of Probate or Grant of Letters of Administration, whilst others have a threshold of about $5,000 to $10,000. One example of exceptional circumstances was the tragic SilkAir Flight 185 crash on 19 December 1997, which killed all 97 passengers and seven crew on board. Some local banks simplified the process of releasing bank account funds to the families of the victims on compassionate grounds.

High net worth individuals (HNWIs) with private banking accounts usually have specially tailored terms that provide for the right of survivorship and other special provisions as to what happens to the funds in the event of death of any of the account holders.

The cause of the myth mentioned above likely arises from confusion, which stems from the mistaken application of the concept of joint tenancy in property law to joint bank accounts.

Joint tenancy is a land law principle that refers to the rights of survivorship in the case of co-owners of immovable property (such as HDB flats, condominiums, etc). It covers the context of two people owning 100% of a property with no distinct shares for each co-owner. Joint tenancy is an operation of property law as opposed to joint back accounts, which are fundamentally a contractual relationship between a customer and the bank, with the contract specifying how the account is to be operated by the customer. Therefore, the right of survivorship does not automatically apply to joint bank accounts, unless it is specified or included in the terms and conditions for the particular joint bank account.

> **Tip**
> Check the terms and conditions of your joint bank account to see if there is a right of survivorship.

For more details on joint tenancy and tenancy-in-common, refer to the previous section in this chapter under "Immovable Property".

Other countries

Countries such as Malaysia, Australia and Hong Kong have similar practices and similar safeguards adopted by banks. As there are differences between banks and between countries, it is prudent to check with your bank in the respective countries.

In Australia, some banks exercise their discretion to make an exception to release funds for funeral expenses on compassionate grounds, if the executor named in the Will can provide an invoice for the funeral expenses. Some banks in other countries make a distinction between owners of funds in joint accounts and owners of funds with signatory rights.

What is worth noting, too, is that most Australian banks have a "threshold amount" for accounts held by deceased persons: if, for example, there is less than say, $50,000 sitting in a deceased person's bank account, they may not require the executor to get a Grant of Probate (especially if it concerns a small estate) and will simply require the executor to sign an indemnity in favour of the bank to enable the bank to release the funds to the estate. Of course, if there is more than the threshold amount, the bank will require the executor to get a Grant of Probate.

> **Tip**
> Check with the bank on who the actual account holder is and the threshold amount.

How do I close a joint bank account?

If the bank informs you that they require the Grant of Probate or Grant of Letters of Administration, you will need to apply to court for this. Once obtained, the executor or administrator must be present at the bank branch for the closure of the account and the release of funds.

Documents required by banks typically include (it is best to check with individual banks for any other requirements):

1. original death certificate;

2. proof of relationship for all beneficiaries (such as marriage or birth certificates);
3. original Grant of Probate or Grant of Letters of Administration sealed in the Singapore court;
4. authorisation for closure of account signed by all executors/administrators; and
5. identity documents of all executors/administrators:
   a. Singaporean/PR: NRIC
   b. Malaysian: Malaysian IC
   c. foreigner: passport

Shares

Public listed shares

Public listed shares traded on the Singapore Stock Exchange (SGX) and held at the Central Depository (CDP) will continue to remain there when the owner dies. The shares can only be sold or transferred once the personal representative of the estate, the executor or administrator, obtains the Grant of Probate or Grant of Letters of Administration that lawfully authorises them to deal with the shares. Once the Grant is obtained, an estate trading account may be opened at the CDP and from there, the shares can be sold or transferred to beneficiaries. In some cases, the shares may not have been updated (they may still be in script form and not converted to scriptless shares) and the executor or administrator would need to check with the share registrar about the status of those shares.

In summary, the first step is for an executor or administrator to obtain the court order, the Grant of Probate or Grant of Letters of Administration. The second step is to open an estate trading account at the CDP with the original Grant.

Private limited shares

If the deceased held shares in a private limited company, the first thing to do is to check with the corporate secretary about the shares belonging to the deceased. Next, consult the corporate secretary or company's lawyer about the company's constitution and if the deceased had signed a shareholder's agreement to check if there is any term that affects the transfer of the deceased's shares. It should be noted that shares will be transmitted in accordance with and subject to the constitution of the company. The transfer process of the shares to the persons legally entitled to them is known as share transmission. It is called a transmission rather than a transfer as what is passed is only the bare legal title and not the beneficial title.

Under clause 28 the Model Constitution, where the sole shareholder of a company dies, only the deceased's personal representative (the executor if the deceased had a valid Will or the administrator if there is no Will) may be recognised by the company as having title to the transmitted shares.

Once transmitted and having obtained the legal title in the shares, the duty of the executor or administrator is to transfer the shares to the lawful beneficiaries. If all the beneficiaries agree, they can consent to the sale of the shares so that the executor or administrator can first sell the shares and then distribute the sale proceeds in the appropriate amounts to the beneficiaries.

Here again, the first step is for an executor or administrator to obtain the court order, the Grant of Probate or Grant of Letters of Administration. The second step is to work with the corporate secretary or company's lawyer to transmit the shares to the executor or administrator, and then transfer the shares to the beneficiaries or have them sold before distributing the sale proceeds, as appropriate.

Insurance

> ### A story of collecting insurance monies
>
> Doug was survived by his wife, Judy. He had one insurance policy which he had bought when he just started working and he did not make a nomination of a beneficiary. Judy made a claim with the insurance company, the company processed the claim and made the payout in favour of Doug's estate. Judy was confused and asked them to make the cheque out in her favour. She was told that as there was no nomination, she was required to produce a Grant of Probate if Doug had a Will, or a Grant of Letters of Administration if he did not, authorising Judy to receive funds on behalf of Doug's estate. The insurance company was entitled to do so at law.

Based on section 61(6) of the Insurance Act (IA),[2] an insurer has the discretion to pay the first S$150,000 of the death proceeds to the "proper claimant". Under the IA, a proper claimant is usually the deceased's immediate family member (such as a spouse, parent, child or sibling), or the executor of a Will or the administrator of the deceased's estate. As this is discretionary, the insurer has the right not to do so and it is not a requirement at law. The practice in Singapore is that the insurer usually makes the initial payout subject to their requirements first being met, and any additional amounts over and above this sum will be paid to the estate of the deceased upon receiving the Grant of Probate or Grant of Letters of Administration.

---

2 Insurance Act (Cap 142, 2002 Rev Ed).

> If you have a Will and you have made a revocable nomination in your insurance policy and you wish to revoke the nomination, you should also make a declaration that you have made a Will providing for disposition of all death benefits under the relevant policy. This is provided for under the Insurance (Nomination of Beneficiaries) Regulations 2009, Form 6.

Nomination of beneficiaries

Under the IA, policyowners can choose to nominate their beneficiaries for their insurance policies at the time a policy is bought or at any time after the policy is issued. After 2009, policyowners have a choice of either a trust nomination under section 49L or a revocable nomination under section 49M of the IA. A revocable nomination allows the policyowner to nominate beneficiaries to receive death proceeds of the policy upon the death of the policyowner. All living benefits will be paid to the policyowner and only the death benefit is payable to the surviving beneficiaries; if there is no surviving beneficiary, the revocable nomination shall be deemed to be revoked.

When the policyowner makes a revocable nomination, the policyowner continues to retain full rights and ownership over the policy. This means that you can change or revoke a nomination at any time without the consent of the beneficiary or beneficiaries. All rights over the policy will be subject to the terms and conditions of the nomination created.

All of the following criteria must be met before a policyowner can consider making a nomination:
  1. The policy must be a life policy or an accident and health policy that provides death benefits, and the

policy must be effected by the policyowner on his or her own life.

2. The policyowner must be at least be 18 years of age to be eligible to make a nomination. If the insurance policy falls under any of the following categories, the nomination of beneficiaries under the IA is not allowed:

   d. Minimum Sum Scheme (MSS);

   e. effected by the policy owner to insure another life assured;

   f. trust policy; and

   g. policy that does not have a death benefit.

Please take note that Muslim policyowners may make either trust or revocable nomination over their life policies or accident and health insurance policies with death benefits.[3]

Comparison between a trust nomination and a revocable nomination:

	Trust Nomination	Revocable Nomination
Does a Will override a nomination?	No	Yes
What happens when my nominee predeceases me?	Proceeds paid to estate of nominee	If there is only one nominee, it is revoked and passes under intestacy or under a Will. Otherwise, the proceeds are shared amongst the surviving nominees.
Can I change my nomination unilaterally?	No. You need the consent of the trustee or all nominees	Yes

---

3 Majlis Ugama Islam Singapura (MUIS) Religious Advisory on Revocable Insurance Nomination for Muslim Policyholders.

> **Note**
>
> 1. If you made a trust nomination for your insurance policy, your Will does not affect that nomination.
>
> 2. If you made a revocable nomination for your insurance policy, your Will can revoke the nomination.

Millions of insurance left unclaimed by families

It has been reported that nearly $2 million has been left unclaimed and the figure has grown since 2001. To facilitate claims, the Life Insurance Association of Singapore launched an online register in 2016 for members of the public to check on unclaimed insurance payouts.

Why is there such a huge sum unclaimed? Apparently, one of the top reasons why life insurance payouts go unclaimed is because beneficiaries of the policies are simply unaware of their eligibility to make such claims. Some people are very private and do not even tell their beneficiaries or next of kin their discreet and secret investments. Unfortunately, as financial advisors who help customers to buy the policies are bound by client confidentiality rules, their lips are sealed and they are unable to help.

A checklist for insurance policies

1. Compile details of all insurance policies.
2. Inform relevant persons so they have knowledge of and easy access to the policies. This includes your loved ones or trustee.
3. Update the details of the policies periodically with your financial advisor.

5

INTESTACY (NON-MUSLIMS) – PASSING AWAY WITHOUT A WILL

There are different distribution rules for non-Muslims and Muslims. This chapter deals with non-Muslim estates. For Muslim estates, see Chapter 8 on Muslim Wills.

When a person dies without a Will, there are two consequences. However, people are usually only aware of one, the distribution of assets. Many are aware of the distribution of shares of assets to beneficiaries under the law. However, the other significant consequence is that there is no named person to carry out the distribution of assets.

> No Will = ~~Personalised distribution plan~~ + ~~Choosing of person to carry out the distribution~~

If you do not make a Will, you are in effect waiving your right to choose:
1. who will manage and distribute your assets; and
2. who your beneficiaries will be and the share of your assets that each of them should receive.

Not specifying either of the above is a significant disadvantage. Not choosing increases the likelihood of disputes.

No Distribution Plan

Not writing a Will has the effect of letting the law write your Will for you, as it provides a pre-planned and fixed distribution scheme depending on who survives the deceased.

This is a list of persons and entities who cannot benefit from your estate if you do not have a Will:

1. your parents, if you are married with lawful children;your stepchildren, if you did not adopt them;
2. illegitimate children and their parents;
3. your life partner, if you are not lawfully married;
4. persons who are not your lawful next of kin, such as godparents, godchildren, friends, etc; and
5. charities and other organisations.

Your parents, if you are married with lawful children

Unlike Malaysia, Singapore intestacy laws do not allow parents to receive a share of the estate if the deceased is survived by both spouse and children or survived only by children. In Singapore, parents can only receive a share if there is no surviving spouse and grandchildren.

Your stepchildren, if you did not adopt them

If Mr A remarries Ms B and Ms B has a lawful child, B1 from her first marriage, B1 is the stepchild of Mr A. B1 is not the lawful child of Mr A, unless Mr A adopts B1. Singapore intestacy laws give the right of entitlement to a child who is legally adopted and the descendants of a deceased's biological child or children. Stepchildren are not entitled, unless they have been legally adopted.

Illegitimate children and their parents

An illegitimate child is one who is born out of wedlock. Singapore intestacy laws give the right of entitlement to a child who is a lawful child or a legitimate child[1] (if the biological parents subsequently marry each other, then that child would be considered legitimated and their lawful child).[2] This means that illegitimate children have no right to inherit from their biological parents. Illegitimate children can only inherit in these cases:

1. If their biological mother did not have other legitimate children, then they can inherit from their mother as if they were a legitimate child.[3]
2. If they become legitimated should their parents subsequently marry.
3. If they become legitimated by one of their biological parents (or other persons) adopting them lawfully.
4. If their biological parents write a Will and appoint them as beneficiaries.

Furthermore, only the biological mother of an illegitimate child has the right to inherit from an illegitimate child if the illegitimate child dies and is survived by the biological mother. The biological father is not entitled to inherit even if he survives the child's death.[4] In a case where an illegitimate child wishes for the biological father to inherit his or her assets, the illegitimate child must write a Will to appoint the biological father as a beneficiary.

If an illegitimate child dies with no surviving spouse, lawful child or parents, it is not entirely clear who will inherit as the Legitimacy Act does not specify and neither does the Intestate

1 Intestate Succession Act (Cap 146, 2013 Rev Ed) s 3.
2 Legitimacy Act (Cap 162, 1985 Rev Ed) s 3.
3 Legitimacy Act, s 10(1).
4 Legitimacy Act, s 10(2).

Succession Act. For such a case, it is once again best to make a Will and also make a nomination for CPF funds to avoid unintended consequences.

Your life partner, if you are not lawfully married

Singapore law does not recognise common law marriages or de facto marriages as in some parts of Australia, Canada and the USA, where a couple may be considered legally married even without formally registering their relationship as a civil or religious marriage. In Singapore, same sex marriages have yet to be recognised as well. The significance is that in such circumstances, the rules of intestacy will prohibit the surviving partner in such relationships from receiving a share of the deceased's assets, unless a Will is made and the life partner is named as a beneficiary. This applies to any benefits that are dependent on the status of a lawful spouse, such as CPF funds and insurance payouts without a nomination.

Persons you do not want to benefit

Without a Will, there are also scenarios where you may have unintended beneficiaries whom you do not wish to benefit from a share of your estate, such as:

1. spouses where the couples intend to separate or divorce, and
2. estranged relatives or next of kin.

There have been instances where one party in an ongoing divorce dies before the completion of the divorce and without making a Will. The deceased's unhappy parents have no right to insist that the soon-to-be ex-spouse is denied a share. This is because under the law, since the divorce was not finalised, the other party remains the lawful spouse. Without a Will, the surviving spouse is entitled to 50% of the late soon-to-be ex-spouse's assets if the couple did not have children, and the parents would be entitled to the other 50% (parents to share equally if both survive).

In other cases, a parent may be estranged from their adult children and the parent has left home for decades. In one such case, the estranged father reappeared and claimed 50% of the assets of the successful deceased son after leaving the family 20 years earlier. The lawful siblings of the deceased had no choice but to accept that their estranged father was entitled to a sizeable portion of the deceased's assets despite doing little for the family.

> No Will = No choice of the person to carry out the distribution

Without a Will, you would have waived your entitlement to choose an executor. The duties of an executor include collecting the assets to pay the lawful debts and taxes, and distributing the residuary assets among the persons entitled. The executor must apply for and be appointed by a court order before he is authorised to carry out his duties.

Without a Will and a named executor, the courts have to go through the process of determining who should be appointed the administrator of the estate or who should have the duties of an executor. The appointment of an administrator of an estate can be contested if there is more than one person entitled to be appointed.

In Singapore, the distribution of assets of a deceased who dies without a Will is governed by the Intestate Succession Act (ISA).[5] Intestacy rules in Singapore differ for non-Muslims and Muslims.

Intestacy Rules of Distribution

(Non-Muslims)

	Singapore	Malaysia
	Intestate Succession Act (Cap 146)	Distribution Act 1958 (West Malaysia and Sarawak) Intestate Succession Ordinance 1968 (Sabah)
Deceased Dies Intestate Leaving	**Distribution**	
Spouse* No Issue** No Parents	Whole share to surviving spouse	Whole share to surviving spouse
Spouse **Issue** No parents	½ share to surviving spouse, ½ share to be shared equally among issue and where they have already died, their children.	½ share to surviving spouse, ½ share to be shared equally among issue and where they have already died, their children.
Spouse **Issue** **Parents**	½ share to surviving spouse, ½ share to be shared equally among issue and where they have already died, their children; **parents are not entitled.**	¼ share to surviving spouse, ¼ share to surviving parents, ½ share to be shared equally among issue and where they have already died, their children.
Issue No Spouse No Parents	Whole share to be shared equally among issue and where they have already died, their children.	Whole share to be shared equally among issue and where they have already died, their children.
Issue **Parents** No Spouse	Whole share to be shared equally among issue and where they have already died, their children. **Parents are not entitled.**	⅓ to be shared equally among surviving parents, ⅔ to be shared equally among issue and where they have already died, their children.

5   Intestate Succession Act (Cap 146, 2013 Rev Ed).

Spouse **Parent** No Issue	½ share to surviving spouse, ½ share to be shared equally among surviving parents.	½ share to surviving spouse, ½ share to be shared equally among surviving parents.
Parents No Spouse No Issue	Whole share to be shared equally among surviving parents.	Whole share to be shared equally among surviving parents.
Siblings No Spouse No Issue No Parents	Whole share to be shared equally among deceased's siblings and where they have already died, their children.	Whole share to be shared equally among deceased's siblings and where they have already died, their children.
Grandparents No Spouse No Issue No Parents No Siblings and their children	Whole share to be shared equally among surviving grandparents.	Whole share to be shared equally among surviving grandparents.
Uncles and Aunts No Spouse No Issue No Parents No Siblings and their children No Grandparents	Whole share to be shared equally among surviving uncles and aunts.	Whole share to be shared equally among surviving uncles and aunts.

Spouse refers to husband or wife.

**Issue* means a child (legitimate or legally adopted) and the descendants of a deceased's child. Illegitimate children and transferred children are not entitled under the intestacy rules.

Presumption that the younger survives the elder

For the purposes of inheritance property, where two or more persons die in circumstances which make it uncertain who died first, it is presumed that the older person died first and, accordingly, the younger shall be deemed to have survived the elder.[6]

Heirless/No Next of Kin

What happens if a person dies leaving no next of kin and no

---

6   Civil Law Act (Cap 43, 1999 Rev Ed) s 30: Presumption of survivorship in regard to claim to property.

Will? This is a case where a person leaves no spouse, children, surviving parents, siblings, grandparents, aunts or uncles. This can happen especially in the case of persons who are illegitimate with no lawful next of kin. What would happen to such a person's assets?

The assets of such persons are known as *bona vacantia*, meaning assets without owners. In the UK, such assets traditionally belong to the Crown. In Singapore, such assets would belong to the Government, which allows claims to be made on the *bona vacantia* estate of a deceased person.

Any person is entitled to make an equitable claim on the *bona vacantia* estate of a deceased if they are able to furnish evidence to support such a claim.

Claims against a bona vacantia *estate*

An equitable claim on a *bona vacantia* estate is made to the Public Trustee.[7] Before a claim can be considered by the Public Trustee, the claimant must prove that the deceased has no surviving next of kin who is eligible to inherit the deceased's property and/or monies under the ISA. As long as there is a lawful next of kin who is entitled, no claim can be made even if such beneficiaries wish to renounce their share in the assets of the deceased.

The Public Trustee considers the following factors:[8]
  1. The length and nature of the relationship between the claimant and the deceased.
  2. Any legal or moral obligations which the deceased had owed the claimant.

---

7 Civil Law Act, s 27(3)
8 Public Trustee's Office website <https://pto.mlaw.gov.sg/deceased-cpf-estate-monies/claims-against-bona-vacantia-estates/>.

3. The claimant's conduct towards the deceased,
   including any contribution to the welfare of the
   deceased.
4. The deceased's last wishes.

The Public Trustee assesses all claims on a case-by-case basis
and decides based on the merits of the evidence for each case
and a claim may not be allowed even if one or more of the above
factors are present as all the circumstances of the case are taken
into consideration.

No claim can be made against a Muslim estate.[9] For Muslim
estates without lawful next of kin, the monies will be paid
to Baitulmal.[10]

The claimant is required to satisfy a waiting period to ensure that
the entitled next of kin has adequate time to make a claim with
the Public Trustee:

Type of Estate (*Bona Vacantia*)	Waiting Period (from date of death)
Estate with movable property, eg bank monies, CPF monies but no immovable property, eg HDB flat, landed property, condominiums	6 months
Estate with immovable property, eg HDB flat, landed property, condominiums	3 years

Inheritance Laws in Asia

Being culturally and religiously diverse, many jurisdictions in
Asia reflect such diversity in their laws relating to inheritance.

9 Civil Law Act, s 27(6).
10 Baitulmal is the institution that acts as a trustee for Muslims. It looks after assets from which
   members of the Muslim public may benefit. In Singapore, the Majlis Ugama Islam Singapura or
   Islamic Religious Council of Singapore (MUIS) administers Baitulmal.

In Malaysia, the primary legislations are the Distribution Act 1958 (West Malaysia and Sarawak) and Intestate Succession Ordinance 1968 (Sabah); in Hong Kong, it is the Intestates' Estates Ordinance (Cap 73). Both jurisdictions have similar intestacy rules as Singapore, but there are differences that should be noted (see table above for a comparison between Singapore and Malaysia for non-Muslims). Indonesia has three inheritance legal systems: *Adat* inheritance law, Islamic inheritance law and Western inheritance law.[11] In the world's most populous democracy of India, there are separate intestacy rules for Hindus, Muslims and Christians.

China's intestacy rules provide two main classes of beneficiaries.[12] The first category of surviving beneficiaries are entitled equally[13] and the second category of other beneficiaries are entitled only if there are no surviving beneficiaries in the first category:

1. Category 1: parents, spouse and children.
2. Category 2: siblings, paternal grandparents and maternal grandparents.

---

11 Yeni Salma Barlinti, "Inheritance Legal System In Indonesia" Year 3 Vol 1, January–April 2013 *Indonesia Law Review*.

12 Law of Succession of The People's Republic Of China (Order No 24 of the President of the People's Republic of China, effective as of 1 October 1 1985) Art 10.

13 Law of Succession of The People's Republic Of China (Order No 24 of the President of the People's Republic of China, effective as of 1 October 1 1985) Art 13.

6

COURT APPOINTMENT TO MANAGE AN ESTATE

Why is a Grant or Court Order Required?

To be able to successfully manage the estate of a deceased, the executor or administrator of an estate *must* be appointed by the court to be lawfully authorised to carry out their roles. Being a court-authorised person secures one of the two keys to manage the assets of the estate.

Power to manage estate assets

Myths

Myth 1: I don't need a Will. The Government, banks and insurance companies will automatically distribute my assets to my family.
Truth: There is no automatic distribution of your assets such as the money in your bank account(s), shares, vehicle, etc.

Myth 2: My Will settles everything and my executor need not do anything more.
Truth: Your Will is advantageous as it appoints your executor and sets out your asset distribution plan to your beneficiaries. However, your executor *must* be authorised by the court in order to be able to manage and distribute your assets.

Most people have the impression that the executor stated in a Will can rely solely on the Will to carry out his/her duties. However, having a Will which appoints an executor is like having one of two keys needed to unlock the power to collect and distribute the assets of the deceased's estate.

The second and lesser-known key, but equally important, is the legal process for appointing a personal representative for the estate. The purpose of the legal process is for the personal representative to be authorised by the court to carry out the duties of the role, such as collecting and distributing the deceased's assets and paying outstanding debts. The legal process leads to a court order that authorises the personal representative to act. The personal representative is known as the executor where there is a Will and the court order is known as a Grant of Probate. The personal representative is known as the administrator where there is no Will and the court order is known as a Grant of Letters of Administration.

> ### Joanna's Will and her bank account
>
> After Joanna's passing, Daniel found her original Will and brought it to the bank to close her account and withdraw the funds. To his surprise, the bank staff explained that they did not require the Will as it was a private document, and even though he was appointed under the Will to be the executor, he had not been appointed and authorised by the court to deal with her assets yet. He learnt that what the bank required was a Grant of Probate as Joanna had made a Will.
>
> Daniel's lawyer explained to him that this was the standard practice for banks and other financial institutions such as insurance companies, and he would help Daniel to apply to the court for the Grant of Probate, before the bank could take instructions from him to transfer the funds and close the bank account. Daniel was relieved to discover that since Joanna had a Will, the process to obtain the Grant (the court order) was a lot quicker and less costly than if there was no Will.

What is a Grant or Court Order?

A Grant of Probate is a court order that appoints a person named in a Will as the executor to manage the estate of the deceased.

Where there is no Will, the court order is known as the Grant of Letters of Administration. In this case, the person appointed by the court is known as the administrator.

Before the court provides such a Grant, it has to be satisfied of various matters, for example, who is the proper applicant, whether credible evidence is furnished of the death of next of kin with prior rights to apply, whether the Will is valid at law and authentic, what the applicable law is and more.

A Grant may be required to be resealed in another country if the executor or administrator wishes to be appointed and authorised to manage the assets located in that other country.

James and a Singapore Grant resealed in Malaysia

James obtained the Grant of Probate for his late father's estate in Singapore as most of his assets were situated in Singapore. His father has two bank accounts in Johor Bahru, Malaysia. James visited the bank branch in Johor Bahru and showed the bank officer the Singapore Grant and was told he needed to obtain a Malaysian Grant before the bank could recognise that he has been duly authorised under the laws of Malaysia. James visited a lawyer in Johor Bahru and was advised that the Singapore Grant had to resealed in the Johor Bahru High Court.

The same would apply if a Grant of Probate was obtained in Malaysia, in that it would have to be resealed in the Singapore High Court if the executor wished to have powers to manage assets in Singapore.

Attached to a Grant is a document known as the Schedule of Assets. This lists all the assets of the deceased's estate. If all the assets are not listed, it may mean that the executor or administrator will not be able to manage the assets that are omitted as the Schedule of Assets is meant to cover all assets to be managed. If an asset is omitted, the executor or administrator may be required to amend the Schedule of Assets for the sake of completeness and to be properly appointed to have the power to manage the omitted asset.

Grant of Probate v Grant of Letters of Administration		
	Grant of Probate	Grant of Letters of Administration
Personal representative	Executor	Administrator
Assets distribution plan	Decided by testator	Rules of intestacy
Appointment of personal representative	Decided by testator	Next of kin entitled to apply, subject to: 1. a ready volunteer; and 2. a priority list and approval by the court.
Additional personal representative	Not necessary	Co-administrator required if there are beneficiaries under the age of 21 or with mental disabilities.
Renunciation by next of kin	Not necessary	Required if there are next of kin with prior and equal priority.
Sureties	Decided by court depending on total value iof estate	Required in cases where beneficiaries are under the age of 21 or with disabilities.
Administration Bond	Not necessary	Required
Cost (legal and court fees)	Lower	Higher, due to more requirements and steps.
Duration to complete	Shorter	Longer, due to more requirements and steps.

Story of a widower with children

Darwin and Emma settled in Singapore a few years ago. Darwin lost his wife, Emma, when the children were in kindergarten. Emma did not have a Will. Darwin could not apply for the Grant of Letters of Administration alone and had to get his best friend, Joseph, to be the co-administrator. Darwin also had to look for sureties to guarantee the children's share of their late mother's estate.

If Emma had made a Will, Darwin could have been the sole executor and there would be no need for Darwin to trouble Joseph or find sureties.

> ### A spinster's story
>
> Madam Lee, an elderly spinster, died leaving behind eight siblings. Her parents and two other siblings had died before her in 1950 and the 1960s, respectively. She was a co-owner of the family shophouse. She did not have a Will. Madam Lee's youngest sibling, Jane, took up the role of settling her estate but ran into many challenges as she could not find the death certificates of her late parents and siblings; she had to arrange for her elderly siblings to attend at the lawyer's office to sign their renunciations and consent to her application to be the sole administrator of the estate, and she also had to find sureties to act as guarantors for the value of the estate. All these additional requirements made Jane's application to the court more cumbersome, time-consuming and costly.
>
> If Madam Lee had made a Will, there would be no court requirement to produce the death certificates, sign renunciations or find sureties, and saved on both time and legal expenses.

Checklist to apply for a Grant:

	Grant of Probate	Grant of Letters of Administration
Death certificate	Deceased	1. Deceased 2. Deceased next of kin with prior and equal rights
Will (Original)	☑	☒
Identity Card/Passport/ Birth certificate	Executor and beneficiary	Administrator Co-administrator Beneficiaries Sureties
List of assets	☑	☑

Roles of Executor and Administrator

The role of the executor or administrator is, generally, to pay the debts of the estate, and collect and distribute the assets according to the law. The duties are similar to that of a trustee and the executor or administrator must act in the interest of the beneficiaries at all times instead of their own. As a trustee, the executor or administrator is accountable to the beneficiaries about the distribution of the assets. In fact, one of the first court documents that the executor or administrator signs under oath is the Administration Oath, which confirms this duty and role as follows:[1]

> I (we) will faithfully administer the estate and effects
> of   deceased by paying his debts so far as his
> estate and effects will extend and the law requires;
>
> I (we) will distribute the residue of his estate and effects
> according to law; and
>
> I (we) will render a just and true account of my (our)
> administration when I (we) am (are) lawfully required.

Estate Bank Account

The executor's bank account

Michael had obtained the Grant of Probate. He managed to close the bank accounts of the deceased and transferred all the monies to his personal bank account for convenience. From his bank account, he paid for the funeral expenses and legal fees. The beneficiaries then asked him for an account of the funds collected and expenses paid. Michael took a long time to differentiate his own expenses from the estate expenses as he had mixed the estate funds with his own funds. He should not have mixed the funds, instead, he should have opened an estate bank account.

---

1   Family Justice Court Practice Directions, Appendix A, Form 54, R/235, Administration Oath.

Story of joint account with executor

Gabriel's mother opened a joint account with him not long before she died. He had intended to use the funds in this joint account to pay her funeral expenses. To his surprise, the bank froze the bank account and he could not access the funds when he informed the bank of her passing. Gabriel and his mother had wanted the convenience of using the joint account and not to bother with opening up a new estate account.

For convenience, parents often add one or more adult children to their bank account as joint account holders. Many parents intend that upon their passing, the joint account holder will use the money in the joint account to pay estate bills, funeral expenses, and ultimately distribute the remaining balance among the estate beneficiaries. However, if the bank freezes the bank account, the joint holder will not be able to use the funds.

An estate account is an account opened after someone has passed away, for the executor or administrator to deposit the deceased person's funds from other assets, such as funds from other bank accounts and sale proceeds of other assets (shares, immovable property, etc), into the estate account. It is from the estate account that the executor/administrator should pay the deceased's debts and from which the estate funds are to be distributed to the beneficiaries.

The main reason to open an estate account is to avoid the mixing of estate funds with an executor's personal funds.

Executors and administrators are under a legal duty to provide an account of the estate funds to all the beneficiaries from the date of death until the date the funds are distributed. If there is no proper written record of collection and payment from the estate funds, the executor or administrator runs the risk of being in breach of his/her duties as a trustee. Having an estate account helps the executor and administrator to fulfil their duties as trustees by keeping a written record with the estate bank account statement of incoming and outgoing funds from whom and to whom.

Rights of Beneficiaries
There are several options available to a beneficiary in the event of a breach of trust by an executor or administrator. Such remedies include claims for damages, injunctions to restrain a breach, tracing and/or recovery of the trust property, criminal prosecution, amongst others.

That said, the most common remedy would be to seek an account from the executor or administrator, as it is often the case that beneficiaries are kept in the dark about the assets of the estate and a good place to start is to know more about it. Once an account is obtained, whether voluntarily or by a court order, the beneficiary can decide on the next course of action, whether to claim damages if he/she has suffered a loss, or to apply for an injunction to stop the executor or administrator from taking further action, or to compel the executor or administrator to take action.

Simple Estates of Less than $50,000 – Public Trustee
If the assets of an estate are worth less than $50,000, the family of the deceased may apply for the Public Trustee (Ministry of Law) to administer the estate, to collect and distribute the assets for a fee payable to the Public Trustee's Office. The Public Trustee will act if *all* of following are satisfied:

1. no disputes among the beneficiaries;
2. deceased has no debts;
3. deceased did not have shares or other interest in unlisted companies (foreign or local);
4. deceased was not a partner or a sole proprietor;
5. deceased was not the sole owner of a HDB flat and a child is eligible to inherit the whole or part of the flat;
6. deceased was not being sued in court;
7. deceased did not have insurance policies where one or more people have been nominated as beneficiaries;[2]
8. deceased did not have trust bank accounts opened with a child; and
9. deceased did not own commercial vehicles such as taxis.

The Public Trustee will not act if any of the above conditions are not met, in which case the family then has the option of appointing a lawyer to obtain the Grant of Administration.

The assets administered by the Public Trustee are:
1. money in banks or other financial institutions in Singapore;
2. shares which are listed on the Singapore Exchange;
3. fully paid-up vehicles, apart from commercial vehicles like taxis;
4. salary the deceased was owed but not yet paid;
5. items in a safe deposit box;
6. money paid as government compensation; and
7. money from the Workfare Income Supplement Scheme.

2 Conveyancing and Law of Property Act (Cap61, 1994 Rev Ed) s73 and Insurance Act (capt142, 2002 Rev Ed) ss49L and 49M.

The Public Trustee's Office helps small estates for a fee as follows:

Value of Estate	Charge
For the first $5,000	6.50%
For the next $2,000	6.00%
For the next $3,000	4.25%
For the next $10,000	2.75%
For the next $30,000	2.25%

In most cases, the executor or intended administrator appoints a lawyer to act for them to make the application to the Singapore Family Court for the Grant of Probate or Grant of Letters of Administration.

Application for Grant

Value of Estate	Less than $50,000		More than than $50,000

- disputes among the beneficiaries;
- deceased has debts;
- deceased has shares or other interest in unlisted companies (foreign or local);
- deceased was a partner or a sole proprietor;
- deceased was the sole owner of a HDB flat and a child is eligible to inherit the whole or part of the flat;
- deceased was being sued in court;
- deceased has insurance policies where one or more people have been nominated as beneficiaries (CLPA s 73 and IA ss 49L & 49M);
- deceased has trust bank accounts opened with a child; and
- deceased owned commercial vehicles such as taxis.

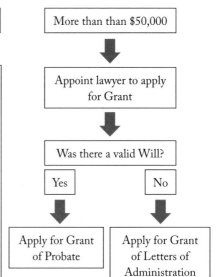

Appoint lawyer to apply for Grant

Was there a valid Will?

Yes / No

Apply for Grant of Probate

Apply for Grant of Letters of Administration

If the answer is "no" to all of the above, you may apply to the Public Trustee to administer the estate – https://eservices.mlaw.gov.sg/pto/welcome.xhtml

If the answer is "yes" to any of the above, you should appoint a lawyer to apply for the Grant.

7

EXECUTORS' DUTIES AND LIABILITIES

The role of the executor or administrator comes with duties and responsibilities. Some of these duties can be onerous and should not be taken lightly. It is therefore important to choose an executor or administrator wisely. Likewise, one should consider carefully before accepting the role of an executor or administrator.

In May 2020, the Family Court held that two women, who were co-executrices of the estate of a deceased woman with a teenage son, were jointly and severally liable to pay about $87,000 to the sole beneficiary, that is the adult son. One of the women was also the guardian of the son after his mother died in 2003. The court found that both women had failed in their duties as joint executrices and trustees of the estate of the deceased.

The district judge found that:[1]

> Both defendants are accountable jointly and severally to the plaintiff. They failed in their duties as joint executrices and trustees of the estate of the plaintiff's mother. It is important to understand that the responsibilities of executors and trustees in general, are onerous. If it cannot be performed, it should not be accepted. Once accepted and not subsequently renounced, then

---

1 *VGV v VGW and VGX* [2020] SGFC 44 at [42]–[43].

liability must be attached when a trustee does little to ensure that the interests of the beneficiaries are secured. It is ever so important in the context of minor beneficiaries.

While the motive of the second defendant in agreeing to assist the plaintiff's mother was unquestionably benevolent, those who seek to assist terminally ill parents who have little choice but to leave the lives and fates of their children in the hands of others, do no justice to those parents if after the show of benevolence, they do nothing. This child had to witness the deaths of both parents. The joint actions of the defendants to advance the trust reposed in them by the testatrix was vitally important to her child. Often in cases where there are two trustees, one may take a backseat but this does mean the law endorses the difference. Being appointed as and accepting the role of an executor typically comes with many responsibilities. The steps involved in performing the duties of an executor may also be lengthy and complex.

Checklist for Executor and Administrator

1. Understand what you need to do
   a. For Executors: Read the Will and understand the deceased's instructions.
   b. For Administrators: Seek legal advice on who are the lawful beneficiaries.
2. Obtain all relevant documents to obtain the Grant:
   a. original death certificate;
   b. original Will (if any);
   c. list of assets;
   d. inheritance certificate (for Muslims).

3. Apply for Grant of Probate within six months of death.

4. Pay off the deceased's debts, taxes and funeral,
    testamentary and administration expenses

    a. If the deceased's estate is solvent (the deceased
        has more assets than liabilities), the executor or
        administrator may use his/her estate to pay off the debts
        and taxes. Under section 58 of the Income Tax Act,[2] the
        executor has to ensure that the deceased's estate is used
        to pay off his income tax liabilities.

    b. If the deceased's estate is insolvent (the deceased's
        liabilities exceed his/her assets), the deceased's funeral,
        testamentary and administration expenses shall have
        priority over any debts or taxes to be paid.

5. Reimbursements (Funeral, Testamentary and
    Administration Expenses)

    a. Section 67 of the Probate and Administration Act
        (PAA)[3] states that if the deceased's estate is worth
        more than $50,000, you may claim from the estate
        a reimbursement of funeral expenses, including all
        reasonable expenses of subsequent religious ceremonies
        performed for the deceased.

    b. If the deceased's estate is worth $50,000 or less, the
        Public Trustee can administer the reimbursement of
        funeral expenses. The maximum amount you may claim
        for funeral expenses is $6,000.

6. Give an account to the beneficiaries

7. Distribute the deceased's assets according to the
    instructions in the Will

---

2   Income Tax Act (Cap 134, 2014 Rev Ed)
3   Probate and Administration Act (Cap 251, 2000 Rev Ed).

Keep proper accounts

As an executor, you are under a fiduciary duty to keep proper accounts and allow the beneficiaries to inspect them as requested at any time. Before the distribution of assets, it is prudent to prepare and share written accounts for the beneficiaries' perusal and approval.

The two-fold purpose of keeping accounts is to:

1. Keep the beneficiaries informed as to the administration and management of the assets of the estate.
2. Have documentary evidence that the executor (or administrator) has performed their duties properly.

Though there are laws or rules on how the accounts should be kept, it would be prudent to keep all written records of collections, payments and transfers to account for each step of administration and management of the assets of the estate.

Distribution of assets

Once you have the Grant of Probate or Grant of Letters of Administration from the court, you may proceed to distribute the assets to the beneficiaries or their respective guardians, according to the terms of the Will or intestacy laws.

The court expects you to administer the estate within a reasonable time of the deceased's death. Generally, it would be prudent to do so within 6 to 12 months from the date of obtaining the Grant.

Section 35(2) of the Conveyancing and Law of Property Act (CLPA)[4] states that no sale of land belonging to the estate of a deceased person shall be made by the legal personal representative(s) of that person after the expiration of six years from his death unless with the sanction of the court. This means that any immovable property may be sold or transferred without a court order if the executor or administrator does so within six years from the date of death. It therefore makes sense to do so within six years of the date of death to avoid a court application to minimise legal fees and time.

Is an executor entitled to be paid?

A testator is at liberty to give a sum of money to the executor for managing and distributing the assets under the Will. However, an executor is entitled to applu under section 66 of the PAA, and the court may, at its discretion, pay the executor a commission of up to 5% of the value of the assets collected.

Powers of Executor and Administrator

The powers and responsibilities of an executor and administrator are as follows.

1. Make any kind of investment, but:
   a. must have regard to standard investment criteria;[5] and
   b. must obtain and consider proper advice.[6]
2. An executor may be given the power of sale by the Will.

   However, a beneficiary may impeach such a trustee if the consideration rendered was inadequate because the condition of sale was unnecessarily depreciatory.[7]

---

4 Conveyancing and Law of Property Act (Cap 61, 1994 Rev Ed).
5 Trustees Act (Cap 337, 2005 Rev Ed) ss 5(1) & 5(3).
6 Trustees Act, ss 6(1) & 6(4).
7 Trustees Act, s 14(1).

3. Seek an order of court for remuneration under section 66(1) of the PAA for commission not exceeding 5% of the value of assets.

4. Be reimbursed for expenses incurred in the course of executing duties under the trust.[8]

5. Administer and call in assets according to the law and with due diligence.[9] A beneficiary may bring a claim against the executor for *devastavit* (the wasting of assets through mismanagement). In such a case, executors must "answer out of their own pockets"[10] and relief may be granted.[11]

6. Settle the lawful debts of the deceased[12] – funeral and testamentary expenses are allowed.[13]

7. Ascertain debts through advertisements to both creditors and beneficial claimants [14] – advertisements must be sufficiently placed.[15]

8. Decide who bears the expenses involved in proving the Will and obtaining the Grant.

9. Render accounts when called upon.[16]

   a. The costs of preparing these accounts are borne by the beneficiary.[17]

   b. Nonetheless, a beneficiary can still apply to the court for an order for the accounts to be furnished.

10. Cost for furnishing estate accounts is paid from the estate.

---

8 Trustees Act, s 59.
9 *Re Tankard, Tankard v Midland Bank Executor & Trustee Co* [1942] 1 Ch 69 at 72.
10 *Ong Wui Swoon v Ong Wui Teck* [2015] SGDC 270.
11 *Re Kay, Mosley v Kay* [1897] 2 Ch 518.
12 Probate and Administration Act, s 57.
13 Probate and Administration Act, s 67.
14 Trustees Act, s 29.
15 *Harrison v Kirk* [1904] AC 1.
16 *Thompson v Dunn* (1870) 5 Ch App 573.
17 *Ottley v Gibly* (1845) 8 Beav 602.

11. Mere delay is insufficient to give rise to liability to pay interest unless it was without good reason – assets should be distributed within a reasonable time.

12. Power of advancement:

    a. Infants may receive maintenance or education advancements if the executor deems it necessary.[18]

    b. This power is in the trustee's absolute discretion so long as it does not prejudice the right of another person.[19]

13. Relieve himself against a claim by making a "Benjamin order": this permits the executor to distribute shares on the basis that certain events may or may not have happened.[20]

14. Beneficiaries may renounce their share in the estate:[21] they can make a disclaimer even before distribution by deed[22] or by conduct.[23]

15. An executor will not be liable after distribution (be granted relief under section 60 of the Trustees Act) so long as:

    a. He/She has acted "honestly and reasonably":[24] reasonably means acting in a way an ordinary intelligent and diligent person would act in his own affairs.[25]

    b. Must also prove that in the circumstances he/she ought fairly to be excused for a breach of trust.[26] However, paid trustees will not be granted relief even if they acted reasonably and with diligence as the standard of care

---

18 Trustees Act, s 34.
19 Trustees Act, s 34(4).
20 *Re Benjamin, Neville v Benjamin* [1902] 1 Ch 723.
21 *Townson v Tickell* (1819) 3 B & Aid 31 at 36.
22 *Re Wimperis, Wicken v Wilson* [1914] 1 Ch 502.
23 *Re Clout & Frewer's Contract* [1924] 2 Ch 230.
24 Trustees Act, s 60.
25 *Re Turner, Barker & Ivimey* [1897] 1 Ch 536; *Wynne v Tempest* (1897) 13 TLR 360.
26 *National Trustees Co of Australasia Ltd v General Finance Co of Australasia Ltd* [1905] AC 373 (PC).

is higher,[27] for example, a trustee who acted on forged letter.[28]

   c. Courts are inclined to favour the executor since it is an office without profit.[29]

16. Sever and apportion any blended trust fund or property.[30]

17. Pay or allow any debt or claim on evidence deemed sufficient.[31]

18. Accept security for any debt or property.[32]

19. Accept payment of debts.[33]

20. Settle accounts or claim relating to the estate.[34]

21. If circumstances require a trustee to obtain insurance, he may be in breach if he does not do so.[35]

22. A civil breach of trust is only proved when there is wilful default.[36]

23. Criminal breach arises when there is dishonesty and an executor or administrator either profited or acquired loss to the estate.[37]

24. Negligence actions may be brought against an executor or administrator, including for committing waste,[38] and beneficiaries can remove the executor or administrator.[39]

---

27 *Barlett v Barclays Bank Trust Co Ltd* [1980] Ch 515; Trustees Act, s 3A.
28 *Re Smith, Smith v Thompson; Smith v Smith* (1902) 71 LJ Ch 411.
29 *Khoo Tek Keong v Ch'ng Joo Tuan Neoh* [1934] MLJ 255.
30 Trustees Act, s 16(1).
31 Trustees Act, s 16(1).
32 Trustees Act, s 16(1).
33 Trustees Act, s 16(1).
34 Trustees Act, s 16(1).
35 *Kingham v Kingham* [1897] 1 IR 170.
36 *Job v Job* (1877) 6 Ch 562 at 564.
37 Penal Code (Cap 224, 2008 Rev Ed) ss 379, 403 & 463.
38 *Royal Brunei Airlines Sdn Bhd v Tan* [1995] 2 AC 378.
39 *Rachel Mei Ling Ong v Dato' Bruno Henry Almeida* [1998] 4 MLJ 268.

Death of Executor

An executor may die before or after the testator (maker) of the Will. Both of these scenarios will be discussed in this section.

Executor dies before testator

If the sole executor dies before the testator and there is no provision in the Will for a replacement executor, then it would be practical for the testator to make a fresh Will appointing a new executor.

If the Will provides for a replacement executor, the replacement executor appointed under the Will may apply to the court to be the executor of the estate when the testator dies.

If all the appointed executors of the Will have died, and there are no replacement executors appointed in the Will, another person can apply to the Family Court to be the administrator of the estate. The administrator applies to the court to be appointed as if they were appointed executor under the Will. The court order granted to this administrator is known as the "Grant of Letters of Administration with the Will Annexed" because there is a Will and it is not the appointed executor applying for the Grant but another person.

Executor dies after testator

If an executor obtains the Grant of Probate and dies, and there are no other executors with a Grant of Probate, then the deceased executor's own executor becomes the executor of the testator's estate with all of his/her rights, duties and responsibilities.[40] However, this does not apply to an executor who does not prove

---

40 Civil Law Act (Cap 43, 1999 Rev Ed) s 25(1).

the Will of his testator and, in the case of an executor who on his own death leaves surviving him some other executor who afterwards proves the Will of that testator, the rule shall cease to apply on such probate being granted.[41] As long as the chain of such representation is unbroken, the last executor in the chain is the executor of every preceding testator.[42] The chain of executorship is broken if the deceased executor left no Will or did not appoint an executor or if no Grant of Probate was granted in respect of his/her Will.[43]

Incapacitated Executor

Due to a lack of mental capacity or physical disability, an executor may be prevented from applying to the court for the Grant of Probate and rendered unable to carry out his/her duties. This often happens when testators do not update their Wills with the result of appointing an executor who is unable to carry out such duties. A typical scenario is when the executor becomes elderly or suffers a serious medical condition and there is no fresh Will to appoint a new executor, especially if there is no suitable replacement executor appointed in the Will.

Fortunately, all is not lost, and the Family Court allows another person to apply for the Grant of Administration with Will Annexed.[44] If the executor has already obtained a Grant of Probate and is subsequently unable to act, a court application is required for the executor to be discharged of his/her duties so that an

---

41 Civil Law Act, s 25(2).
42 Civil Law Act, s 25(3).
43 Civil Law Act, s 25(4).
44 Rule 231 of the Family Justice Rules states that where a relevant person entitled to a Grant is, by reason of lack of mental incapacity and is incapable of managing himself/his affairs, administration for his use and benefit may be granted (a) in the case of lack of capacity (i) to the person authorised by the court; or (ii) to the donee authorised to make decisions about the relevant person's affairs under a LPA; or (b) where there is no person so authorised, if the relevant person is entitled as executor, to the person to the residuary estate of the deceased (formerly Rules of Court O 71 r 29).

administrator can be appointed. If the incapacitated executor has yet to apply for the Grant of Probate, the replacement executor or any other person may apply to the court for the Grant of Letters of Administration with Will Annexed to be appointed as administrator of the estate.

Tips

1. Appoint at least one replacement executor in your Will.

2. Review your Will regularly and be aware of the health of your executor(s).

3. Update your Will if any of your executors die.

Claim for Reasonable Financial Provision against Estate

Can a person who has been left out as a beneficiary under a Will make a claim against the estate? Can a beneficiary ask for more than what he or she was provided for under a Will? Such claims may be made against an estate and it is usually the executor who is the defendant in such a legal action.

In the case where there is no reasonable provision for maintenance of the following persons under the Will, they may apply to the court under the Inheritance (Family Provision) Act (IFPA):[45]

1. a spouse;
2. a daughter who has not been married or who is, by reason of some mental or physical disability, incapable of maintaining herself;
3. a son under 21 years of age; or
4. a son who is, by reason of some mental or physical disability, incapable of maintaining himself.

45 Inheritance (Family Provision) Act (Cap 138, 1985 Rev Ed) s 3(1).

The IFPA was enacted not for the purposes of constraining a person's ability to dispose of his assets under his Will but for the reasonable maintenance of that person's dependants during the lifetime of such dependants.[46] The court would not want to interfere with what would normally be a testator's privilege to dispose of his own money in his own way, and the IFPA is, therefore, limited to the provision of *reasonable maintenance* and not for obtaining legacies out of a testator's estate.[47]

Professor Monteiro's Case

In 1997, Jeanne Christine Monteiro, with the help of her sister Hyacinth Irene Monteiro, sued her father's estate under section 3 of the IFPA.[48] She wanted reasonable financial provision to be made and paid out of the net assets of her deceased father's (Professor Ernest Steven Monteiro's) estate.

Jeanne was 61 years old, unmarried and had a history of schizophrenia since her youth. Professor Monteiro had remarried. He made his new wife, Ling Mie Hean, and her brother the executors of his estate in his Will. When the professor died on 2 March 1989, he left his entire estate to his new wife and the son he had with her.

Choo Han Teck JC as he then was held that Jeanne was qualified to make the application by virtue of her being a spinster alone, but also held that "[i]n this case, the testator had clearly made reasonable provisions for the Plaintiff albeit not by way of his will."[49] Choo JC went on to decide that that there was no justification to grant the application.

---

46 *AOS v Estate of AOT* [2011] SGHC 23.
47 *APZ v AQA* [2011] SGHC 94.
48 *Jeanne Christine Monteiro v Ling Mie Hean* [1997] SGHC 296.
49 *Jeanne Christine Monteiro v Ling Mie Hean* [1997] SGHC 296 at [11].

The professor had given Jeanne a house as a joint tenant with her sister, Hyacinth, which was worth about $4 million at the date of the court application. The net assets of the professor's estate was about $58,942.31. Choo JC also held that if a testator had made adequate *inter vivos* provisions (provisions made during the testator's lifetime) for the persons entitled under section 3(1), the court should not interfere with his right to determine who should have the benefit of his estate. In this case, the provision of maintenance for Jeanne made by the professor when he was still alive was not only subsisting but had appreciated in value many times over. Even if the court found that the testator had not made reasonable provision in his Will for a person qualified under sections 3(1)(*a*) to 3(1)(*d*), the decision to intervene was still discretionary.

Sadly, as with many family disputes, Choo JC observed:[50]

> It is clear from the affidavits of Hyacinth Irene Monteiro that she harbours a deep resentment of Ling Mie Hean. She scorns the perceived inadequacy of the latter in expressing herself in English and even criticised the grammar on Professor Monteiro's tombstone erected by her. While the animosity exists and is apparent from the affidavits filed by Hyacinth Irene Monteiro I do not think that it is of any significant consideration in this case.

Ex-wife's claim for autistic son

In another case, a mother, MC, sued MB's (her ex-husband's) estate as she felt that what was left to their young son was not enough.[51] MC, 34, was married to MB, 68. MB divorced MC

---

50 *Jeanne Christine Monteiro v Ling Mie Hean* [1997] SGHC 296 at [10].
51 *APZ v AQA* [2011] SGHC 94.

three years after being married.[52] In the divorce proceedings, District Judge Laura Lau, amongst other things, ordered the following (the 2005 Order):

1. lump sum maintenance of $20,000 to the mother, MC;
2. monthly sum of $650 as maintenance for the son; and
3. a sum of $21,478.44, being the net sale proceeds of the matrimonial flat, to be divided equally between MB and the mother, MC.

MC appealed, asking, amongst other things, for a lump sum maintenance of $200,000 for the son, and a lump sum maintenance of $30,000 for herself. Justice Tan Lee Meng dismissed MC's appeal on 25 January 2006.

Later in 2006, MC tried to vary the 2005 Order, seeking:

1. MB to pay maintenance for the son at $2,500 per month, alternatively, a lump sum of $250,000 for the son; and
2. MB to pay the mother a sum of $1,000 per month, alternatively, a lump sum of $100,000.

This was dismissed by District Judge Khoo Oon Soo on 11 November 2006, and the appeal was dismissed by Justice Tay Yong Kwang.[53]

In 2008, MC applied for lump sum maintenance of $250,000 for both her son and herself.

---

52 *MB v MC* [2005] SGDC 181.

53 Justice Tay made no order as to costs. In his ruling, Justice Tay cautioned MC about future costs orders if she persisted in taking out unmeritorious applications and appeals (*MB v MC* [2008] SGHC 246 at [7]).

District Judge Regina Ow dismissed the application and MC's appeal was also dismissed by Justice Woo Bih Li.[54]

Despite all that had happened, MB gave gifts of cash of $10,000 to the son and $5,000 to the mother by his Will made in 2008. The residue of the estate, after payment of MB's debts, funeral and testamentary expenses, was to be divided between MB's two daughters in equal shares. MB died on 23 January 2009.

MC believed that $10,000 was grossly insufficient for her autistic son. The mother applied under section 3(1)(c) of the IFPA for an order that reasonable provision for the son's maintenance be made out of MB's estate. Justice Belinda Ang dismissed this application. Justice Ang explained that if the court made an order under the IFPA, "the court would be invading or interfering with what would be normally a testator's privilege to dispose of his own money in his own way".[55] The purpose of the IFPA was thus limited to the provision of reasonable maintenance and not for the purpose of obtaining legacies out of the testator's estate. Outside of section 3(4), the IFPA did not provide for any lump sum payment, and the court was not empowered to make such an order. For the maintenance of a beneficiary, this could be made under section 3(1), and only out of the net estate by way of periodical payments.

A widow's tale

A widow applied for maintenance for herself and on behalf of one of their married adult children, S. The estate opposed the application. In this case,[56] the testator made his Will on 3 April

---

54 *MB v MC* [2008] SGHC 246.
55 *APZ v AQA* [2011] SGHC 94 at [14].
56 *AOS v Estate of AOT* [2011] SGHC 23.

2006 and died on 22 August 2006. He gave all his property to his grandson, G. The widow and S resided in one of those properties with G at the time of the application.

It was undisputed that the testator did not make any provision for the widow in the Will. The estate suggested this was expected in the light of the conflicts within the family at the time the testator made the Will. The estate also contended that the testator had, during his lifetime, made provisions for both the applicant and S through gifts of real property in India to S, and S and the testator jointly, which were worth about $2 million. The widow also owned other real property in India, and was receiving a monthly income of at least $12,000 from rent and $5,000 from the testator's family in India. This exceeded her claimed monthly expenses (excluding accommodation) of $9,443.

Justice Lee Seiu Kin held that the Act was enacted not for the purposes of constraining a person's ability to dispose of his assets under his Will but for the reasonable maintenance of that person's dependents during the lifetime of such dependents. This much is clear from the following provisions of section 3:
1. subsection (2), which provides that the maintenance shall, in the case of a spouse, cease upon remarriage;
2. subsections (3) and (4), which constrain the funds to come from the income of the net estate except where the net estate is less than $50,000; and
3. subsection (5), which prohibits a realisation of any asset that would be disadvantageous to the beneficiaries under the Will.

Justice Lee held that the Act provided for the reasonable maintenance of the testator's dependents. To that extent, the applicant was a dependent and if the testator's Will did not make any provision for her, then the court had the power to make such order as it deemed reasonable for the maintenance of the dependent, out of the income of the net estate.

Justice Lee took into account that during his lifetime, the testator had vested in the applicant a number of properties out of which she was presently deriving at least about $12,000 in monthly income. This amount was more than the sum of some $9,443 that the widow had stated in her supporting affidavit as her monthly expenses, apart from accommodation. Since the widow was residing with her son and his family at the indicated property with G, the beneficiary under the Will, it appeared to the court that the most convenient and practical order in the circumstances would be that the executors continued to provide her with accommodation with G, provided she lived with him until he reached the age of 21. If the executors then decided to sell the property and provide a replacement home for G, they were to provide suitable accommodation for the applicant as well in the replacement home. Justice Lee was of the view that such an order would satisfy the applicant's rights under the Act while preserving the rights of the beneficiary to the Will.

8

MUSLIM WILLS

Muslim Inheritance Law

In Singapore, the Muslim or Syariah law applies to Muslims in personal matters such as marriage, divorce and inheritance. The Syariah Court is a specialised court that decides such matters as set out under the Administration of Muslim Law Act (AMLA),[1] including issuing the inheritance certificate for Muslims estates.[2]

The rules which apply to Muslims are very different from the rules that apply to non-Muslims. AMLA provides that the assets of a deceased Muslim who was domiciled in Singapore at the time of death are to be distributed in accordance with the principles of Muslim law and, where applicable, Malay customs.[3]

Nothing in AMLA shall be held to prevent any Muslim person directing by his or her Will that his or her estate and effects are to be distributed according to Muslim law.[4] Furthermore, nothing in section 111 of AMLA shall affect the provisions of the Wills Act (WA),[5] other than section 3 of the WA; the provisions of the Insurance Act (IA);[6] the provisions of the Probate and

---

1 Administration of Muslim Law Act (Cap 3, 2009 Rev Ed) (AMLA).
2 AMLA, s 115.
3 AMLA, s 112.
4 AMLA, s 110.
5 Wills Act (Cap 352, 1996 Rev Ed).
6 Insurance Act (Cap 142, 2002 Rev Ed).

Administration Act (PAA);[7] or the Will of a Muslim who died before 1 July 1968.

After 1 July 1968, no Muslim domiciled in Singapore is to dispose of his/her property by Will except in accordance with the provisions of and subject to the restrictions imposed by the school of Muslim law professed by him.[8] Subject to section 111 of AMLA, Muslim married women may, with or without the concurrence of their husbands, by Will dispose of their own property.[9]

The Syariah law on inheritance which determines the manner and order of distribution of the assets of a deceased Muslim is known as *Faraidh*. The principles of *Faraidh* are based on the Holy Quran. *Faraidh* is generally applied to the assets of a deceased Muslim, except for assets that have been given away under the deceased's Will (*Wasiat*) and other "excluded" assets.

The Majlis Ugama Islam Singapura (MUIS)[10] was established as a statutory body in 1968 when AMLA came into effect. One of the principal functions of MUIS is to offer religious guidance to the Muslim community in all aspects, including Wills. Muslims are encouraged to write a Will. The reason is the same as for anyone who makes a Will – to avoid conflicts to beneficiaries, for ease of administration and to minimise legal expenses and the time taken to settle an estate.

However, in addition to the basic requirements of a Will set out by the WA,[11] a Muslim Will must also satisfy the following:

---

7   Probate and Administration Act (Cap 251, 2000 Rev Ed).
8   AMLA, s 111.
9   AMLA, s 118.
10 MUIS is also known as the Islamic Religious Council of Singapore.
11 See Chapter 3.

1. It must be witnessed by two male Muslims, who are not the beneficiaries.
2. The amount to be given away under the Will must not be more than one third of the total assets.
3. The beneficiaries of the Will must not be any of the heirs (who will receive their share under *Faraidh*).

It is, therefore, useful for a Muslim to decide how much, up to one third of their assets, to distribute under a Will. This is more advantageous than having all of the assets' distribution restricted by *Faraidh*. Another big advantage of making a Will is that a Muslim is able to choose and appoint an executor under his/her Will, and therefore be able to avoid the cumbersome and more expensive task of applying for a Grant of Letters of Administration.

What is Covered under a Muslim Will?

All of a deceased's assets are subject to *Faraidh,* including cash, jewellery, land, shares, stocks, bonds, motor vehicles, etc. Property held in a joint tenancy or assets which are subject to the deceased's Will *(Wasiat)* may be excluded from distribution in accordance with the rules of *Faraidh*.

The distribution rules of *Faraidh* can be varied when all of the deceased's beneficiaries *(Waris)* agree to distribute the deceased's assets in an alternative way, for example, in equal proportions among all of them. This is usually accomplished with the use of what is sometimes referred to as the "Letter of Wishes". By doing so, distribution according to *Faraidh* may be varied, as long as all the legal beneficiaries consent to the arrangement.

The consent of the legal beneficiaries has the effect of modifying the application of the distribution of the estate under *Faraidh*. This, however, is still subject to the restrictions within *Faraidh* to ensure that disposable assets under a Muslim Will are limited to one third of the estate. The effect of the intervention or introduction of the consent together with the adoption of the Letter of Wishes of a testator has been the subject of a recent court decision.[12]

In a Muslim estate in Singapore, the consent to be obtained from a *Faraidh* beneficiary or beneficiaries will typically allow the legal beneficiary's share entitlements to be distributed according to the wishes of the consenting beneficiaries. This may typically again refer to the whole estate or to two-thirds of the estate, in the latter event where the disposable third of the estate is distributed under a Will.

Legal Consequences of Contravening *Faraidh*

For Muslims in Singapore, compliance with *Faraidh* is mandatory under Singapore law, and legal action can be taken against the administrator or executor of a deceased Muslim's estate or anyone who manages or administers the deceased's assets in breach of *Faraidh*. A person in breach may face legal action in court to account for or make good the breach. If a Muslim makes a Will that breaches the rules of *Faraidh*, that document may be held to be invalid by the court.[13]

Situations where *Faraidh* does not Apply

Faraidh applies only to the assets of a deceased who was a Muslim at the time of his/her death and to the deceased's beneficiaries

---

12 *Husain Safdar Abidally v Shiraz Safdar Abidally* [2006] 4 SLR 800.
13 *Mohamed Ismail Bin Ibrahim v Mohd Taha Bin Ibrahim* [2004] 4 SLR 756.

(Waris) who were Muslims at the time of the deceased's death. *Faraidh* does not apply to a deceased who had renounced Islam during his/her lifetime and who had died a non-Muslim. There is no right of inheritance under *Faraidh* as between a Muslim and a non-Muslim. A beneficiary of a deceased Muslim cannot inherit from the deceased under *Faraidh* if the beneficiary has renounced Islam and is a non-Muslim at the time of the deceased's death.

Persons Eligible to Inherit from a Deceased Muslim

There are generally two classes of beneficiaries: Quranic heirs (*Ashabul furud*) and residual beneficiaries (*Asabah*).

For Quranic heirs, there are twelve heirs with fixed shares mentioned in the Quran:
1. Husband
2. Wife
3. Father
4. Mother
5. Grandfather
6. Grandmother
7. Daughter
8. Son's Daughter
9. Full Sister
10. Sister from the same father (Consanguine sister)
11. Sister from the same mother (Uterine sister)
12. Brother from the same mother (Uterine brother)

Practical reasons for a Muslim Will

There is some confusion over whether Muslims can or cannot or do not have to do a Will since the rules of *Faraidh* apply to them.

On the contrary, Muslims are allowed to make a valid Will and distribute up to one-third (⅓) of their estate according to their Will. The following are some situations where it may be good to do so:

1. there is a non-Muslim beneficiary;
2. there is an adopted child beneficiary;
3. appointment of an executor; and
4. appointment of a testamentary guardian.

Non-Muslim beneficiary

Non-Muslims cannot be lawful beneficiaries under a Muslim estate under *Faraidh*. Muslims are allowed to make a Will and make a non-Muslim one of the beneficiaries in the Will. This would be important if you have a non-Muslim person whom you wish to make a lawful beneficiary.

Adopted child

Under *Faraidh*, an adopted child is not a lawful beneficiary. Making a Will allows a parent to give the lawfully adopted child up to one-third (⅓) of the estate.

Appointment of executor

A Will allows a Muslim to choose and appoint his/her choice of executor, who will manage, administer and distribute the assets after the testator dies. If there is no appointment of an executor, the law will step in to make the choice, which may not be the best choice for the family.

Appointment of guardian for children
One significant benefit for parents with children is that making a Will allows one to choose and appoint a person to be the lawful guardian in the event of the parents' death and the children have not attained the age of 21. The lawful guardian is known as a testamentary guardian who will have the lawful power to make decisions for the children as if he/she is the lawful parent, such as enrolling and registering the children for school, signing school consent forms, opening bank accounts and being responsible for their welfare and care.

Portion of each beneficiary's share
Generally, spouses and immediate family receive higher shares. Moreover, each man receives twice the share of a woman of the same relational level. For example, a son will receive twice the share of a daughter. However, the exact calculation of shares depends very much on the circumstances of each case. To get a better idea, refer to the online *Faraidh* calculator provided by the Syariah Court.

A beneficiary may be disqualified from receiving his/her share under certain circumstances:
1. if he/she has caused the death of the deceased;
2. if he/she is not Muslim; or
3. if he/she has renounced Islam.

Management and Distribution of Assets for a Muslim Estate
1.   Application for inheritance certificate
The first step is to apply for an inheritance certificate from the

Syariah Court. The inheritance certificate is a certificate showing the valid beneficiaries and the shares to which they are entitled under *Faraidh*.

Steps to apply for an inheritance certificate on the online application portal:

1. Make an undertaking that you are a qualified person or body requesting an inheritance certificate – qualified persons or bodies include a beneficiary or a law firm.
2. Input the deceased's personal particulars.
3. Enter the beneficiaries' personal particulars.

The certificate will then show who the valid beneficiaries are and their respective shares.

The inheritance certificate should be ready for collection in person at the Syariah Court after three working days. The original death certificate and the NRIC/passport of the applicant and the beneficiaries are required for the collection of the inheritance certificate.

2.   *Application for Grant of Probate or Grant Letters of Administration*

The second step is to apply to the Family Court for a Grant of Probate or Letters of Administration. This will allow the court to appoint someone to manage and distribute the deceased's estate.

In all applications for Probate or Letters of Administration, the affidavit supporting the application also requires, in the case of a

deceased Muslim, indication of the school of law (*Mazhab*) which
the deceased professed in addition to the particulars required by
any other written law.[14]

3. Distribution of estate

Where a deceased made a Will, the Grant of Probate authorises
the appointed executor to administer and distribute the deceased's
estate in accordance with the Will. Where a deceased died
intestate without a Will, the Grant of Letters of Administration
authorises the appointed administrator to administer and
distribute the deceased's estate according to *Faraidh*.

In granting Letters of Administration to the estate of a Muslim
who dies intestate, the court may, if it thinks fit, grant Letters of
Administration to any next of kin of the deceased Muslim or any
other person entitled to a share in the estate under Muslim law.[15]

No Heirs or Lawful Next of Kin

For Muslim estates without lawful next of kin, monies will be
paid to Baitulmal. Baitulmal is the institution that acts as a
trustee for Muslims. It looks after assets from which members of
the Muslim public may benefit. In Singapore, MUIS administers
Baitulmal. Children born out of lawful Islamic marriages do not
have the right to inherit from the father. However, they are able
to inherit from the mother's estate.[16]

For illegitimate children generally, see Chapter 5.

---

14 AMLA, s 113.
15 AMLA, s 116.
16 MUIS.

Application for Grant – Muslim Estate

Value of Estate	Less than $50,000		More than than $50,000

If answer is "no" to all of the following:
- disputes among the beneficiaries;
- deceased has debts;
- deceased has shares or other interest in unlisted companies (foreign or local);
- deceased was a partner or a sole proprietor;
- deceased was the sole owner of a HDB flat and a child is eligible to inherit the whole or part of the flat;
- deceased was being sued in court;
- deceased has insurance policies where one or more people have been nominated as beneficiaries (CLPA s 73 and IA ss 49L & 49M);
- deceased has trust bank accounts opened with a child; and
- deceased owned commercial vehicles such as taxis.

The Public Trustee will distribute the estate of a Muslim in line with AMLA s 112 and the Certificate of Inheritance issued by the Syariah Court that lists down the beneficiaries and their share of the inheritance.

If the answer is "yes" to any of the above, you should appoint a lawyer to apply for the Grant.

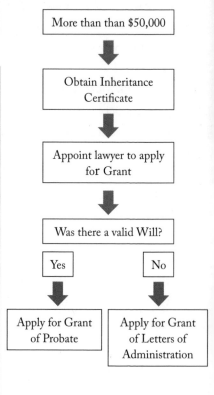

Obtain Inheritance Certificate

Appoint lawyer to apply for Grant

Was there a valid Will?

Yes

No

Apply for Grant of Probate

Apply for Grant of Letters of Administration

9

ESTATE DUTY AND OTHER TAXES

Beneficiaries can be affected by tax in unexpected ways if there is a lack of planning and if the deceased did not make a Will to plan accordingly, ensuring that tax would not be imposed. The common types of tax include Estate Duty, Buyer's Stamp Duty (BSD), Seller's Stamp Duty (SSD) and Additional Buyer's Stamp Duty (ABSD).

Estate Duty

Estate duty has been removed in cases where the date of death is on or after 15 February 2008. However, it is still applicable where the deceased died before that date. In some cases, where the estate has not been settled, estate duty may be payable and interest on the estate duty continue to accrue from the date of death.

Estate duty is a tax on the total market value of a person's assets (cash and non-cash) at the date of his or her death. It does not matter if the person has made a Will or not. The deceased's assets are still subject to estate duty. The deceased's assets, as a whole, are called an estate. For the majority of estates, there is no estate duty payable as various exemptions are provided.

In Malaysia, estate duty was abolished in 1991.[1] Currently,

---

1 As of 1 November 1991.

Singapore and Malaysia do not have any form of death tax, estate duty or inheritance tax. This means that both countries do not impose a final tax on the accumulated wealth of a deceased individual. Indonesia, Myanmar, Cambodia and Laos also do not impose estate duty. However, the Philippines, Thailand, Vietnam and Brunei do impose estate duty.

Other Taxes

Although no tax is imposed when assets are given to a beneficiary under a Will or according to the rules of intestacy, there are situations where tax can be payable if there is a distribution of assets that deviates from the Will or the rules of intestacy.

In the usual property transaction involving the buying and selling of HDB or private property, the Inland Revenue Authority of Singapore (IRAS) imposes BSD, SSD and ABSD where applicable. The liability to pay such taxes by beneficiaries may arise in situations where there is a re-distribution of such immovable assets under the estate that is not in accordance with the Will, intestacy rules or Muslim *Faraidh* laws of inheritance.

A story of re-distribution and paying tax

Jacob did not leave a Will and he owned a condominium apartment in his sole name. He was survived by his wife, Rachael, and four sons, Reuben, Simon, Joseph and Benjamin. Rachael is entitled to 50% of the apartment and the four sons each have an equal share in the remaining 50%. The three older sons have apartments of their own and Benjamin was planning to apply for a HDB flat with his fiancée. The four sons decided to renounce their share in the condominium apartment and give their respective shares to their mother. Rachael would be liable to BSD on the transfer of her sons' shares to her.

> If Jacob had made a Will, he could have given the apartment to Rachael and his family would not have to pay the stamp duty. Rachael and her four sons should see their lawyer to prepare a Deed of Family Arrangement for the sons to renounce their rights and give their shares to their mother.

If there is a re-distribution of shares in immovable property resulting in a transfer of beneficial ownership to another, the prevailing stamp duty rates will apply.

Where there is a change in beneficial interest in a property by way of gift, including a settlement, full stamp duty (BSD, ABSD or SSD, whichever is applicable) will be payable where the distribution is not in accordance with the Will, intestacy rules or Muslim *Faraidh* laws of inheritance.

Transfer of HDB flats amongst family members
Before 2008, stamp duty was applicable for all transfers of HDB flats. Since 2008, BSD and SSD remission may be applicable for the transfer of a HDB flat to a family member, if the remission conditions are met.[2]

The IRAS rules for remission of stamp duty are as follows:
1. The incoming lessee, if any, is a member of any remaining lessee's immediate family and is a Singapore Citizen or a Singapore Permanent Resident.
2. No consideration is provided except for the repayment to the outgoing lessee's Central Provident Fund account.

---

2 Stamp Duties (Transfer of HDB Flat within Family) (Remission) Rules 2007 (S 735/2007).

3. At least one of the existing lessees remains as a lessee of the flat after the transfer has taken place and the remaining lessee is a person who had:

   a. acquired the flat and paid stamp duty on the acquisition;

   b. acquired the flat via mutual exchange and paid stamp duty on the exchange;

   c. acquired the flat by way of assent or distribution or pursuant to a Will; or

   d. acquired the flat via the right of survivorship as a joint tenant upon the demise of another joint tenant.

A story of a brother giving up his share

Mary was the sole owner of a HDB flat. She was survived by two sons, Joshua and James, who were entitled to a half share each. Joshua wanted to retain the HDB flat in his sole name and James was agreeable. Essentially, James agreed to give Joshua his 50% share. Under the IRAS remission rules, Joshua did not have to pay BSD as he met the conditions for remission.

IRAS requires written confirmation from HDB that the incoming lessee will form a family nucleus with the remaining lessee and the incoming lessee is authorised to stay in the HDB flat by HDB. If there is no incoming lessee, the confirmation from HDB is not required.

It is important to note that this remission of stamp duty does not apply to private property.

Estate Income

If the assets left by a deceased person continue to produce income after his death, this income is referred to as estate income. Estate income refers to the income derived from a day after the date of death until the end of the administration period, when the assets are sold or transferred. Estate income is subject to income tax.

Estate Duty v Income Tax on Estate Income	
Tax on the total market value of a person's assets as at the date of his or her death.	Tax on the income earned from a deceased's assets from the day after the date of death until the assets are sold or transferred.

Trust Income

Where an executor holds assets of an estate under a testamentary trust created by a Will, or an administrator holds the same as trustee under an intestate estate, and the assets held by such trustees produce income, such trust income may be liable to tax.

Common examples of assets that generate estate and trust income are:

1. rental income from immovable property;
2. interest from bank/finance company (including POSB);
3. share of profit from a partnership;
4. profit from a sole proprietorship business;
5. dividends from shares declared after death (excluding exempt/one-tier dividends);
6. director's fee and non-contractual bonuses declared after death;
7. income distributions from Unit Trusts/Real Estate Investment Trusts (REITS);
8. gains from share options exercised after death;

9. royalties;

10. foreign-sourced income remitted into Singapore; and

11. other gains or profits of an income nature.

FREQUENTLY ASKED QUESTIONS

Below are answers to some commonly asked questions relating to Wills, to clear doubts and clarify some basic misconceptions about Wills. Any queries that are not addressed here should be directed to a suitable professional like a lawyer.

1. **If I do not have a lot of assets and my family members are not acrimonious, why should I make a Will?**

   It makes sense to have a Will as your next of kin is still required to be lawfully appointed by a court order (known as a Grant) in order to be authorised to manage your estate, which is cheaper and quicker to obtain if you have made a Will.

2. **What happens if I do not have a Will?**

   The law will decide who your beneficiaries will be and the share that each will get under the laws of intestacy. In the application to obtain a court order to be lawfully appointed to manage the assets in your estate, your next of kin will take more time to complete the court process and it will cost more if you do not have a Will.

3. **Must I inform my family members if I have made a Will?**

   You are not required to inform your family members as you are entitled to decide who should know about your

Will and whether they should know the contents. More importantly, the executor of your Will should know where to locate it.

4. **What is the difference between a Will and a Trust?**
    The primary purpose of a Will is to appoint your executor to carry out your wishes in the Will and to distribute your assets to your beneficiaries as specified. A trust is a legal method of appointing a trustee to hold your assets for the benefit of your beneficiaries.

5. **What is the difference between a Will and a Lasting Power of Attorney (LPA)?**
    A Will sets out the distribution of your assets to your beneficiaries upon your death and appoints an executor to carry out the duty of distributing according to your Will. An LPA appoints a person to take on the power to make decisions on your behalf (on medical and financial matters) when you are alive but lack mental capacity to do so yourself. An LPA can only be used in Singapore.

6. **How does one start to make a Will?**
    You should start by considering:
    a. Who should be the executor(s) of your Will to ensure that your wishes are carried out.
    b. Who should be the beneficiaries under your Will.
    c. Who you would like to act as the guardian(s) for any child(ren) under 21, to make decisions regarding their upbringing, education and general welfare.
    d. Whether you want to exclude anyone who would normally be provided for in your Will.

7. **What if I am not able to find a suitable executor from amongst my relatives and friends?**

   Ideally, you should appoint a family member or a trusted friend. If you are not able to do so, you may need to appoint a professional to take on this role, which will incur fees.

8. **What if my beneficiary predeceases me?**

   The gift to the beneficiary will lapse and you should update your Will if there are no provisions in your Will to give that gift to another beneficiary.

9. **Who will ensure an executor carries out the wishes set out in a Will accordingly?**

   An executor's duty is to act in the best interest of the beneficiaries and he/she will be liable to the beneficiaries. The beneficiaries have a legal right to seek an explanation from the executor for his/her conduct.

10. **Who will hold an executor liable if he/she fails to distribute the estate according to the terms of the Will?**

    The persons who can hold an executor liable are the beneficiaries if the executor does not carry out his duties in accordance with the Will or as the law requires. If a beneficiary is a minor, an adult can be appointed to act on behalf of the minor.

11. **Who needs to be present for the execution of a Will?**

    Only the maker of the Will needs to be present and the office of the lawyer preparing the Will would usually provide the witnesses. Your beneficiaries do not need to be present nor does your executor.

12. **What are the duties of an executor, trustee and guardian?**

Basically, an executor collects and distributes the assets of the estate and pays off any debts, a trustee holds assets for the beneficiaries until transferred to the beneficiaries at a specified time, and a guardian has the power to exercise parental responsibilities for a child or children under the age of 21.

13. **I have a joint bank account with my husband. If I pass on, will all the money in the account automatically go to my husband?**

Whether the bank will allow the joint account holder to have access to the money or close the account depends on the terms and conditions set by the bank for that account. You can also clearly express in your Will your intentions for the money in the account.

14. **Can I have charitable organisations as my beneficiaries?**

Yes, the organisations just need to be clearly identified. You should also seek the advice of a lawyer if you have specific instructions about the use of the funds to be given to the organisations.

15. **What is a "basic" will?**

There is no legal definition for a "basic" Will, but a Will that has only one executor and one beneficiary can be considered basic. The more important consideration is to have a Will that is clear and comprehensive.

16. **What happens to my Will if I get married or divorced?**

A Will is revoked upon marriage, but not on divorce. If you have not made a Will or made one before marriage and you now intend to divorce, you should make a Will immediately if you do not wish the rules of intestacy to apply and if you do not wish your spouse to have priority to apply for the Grant of Letters of Administration.

17. **What is considered immovable properties in a Will?**
Immovable property refers to real property or real estate, such as a flat, apartment or landed property.

18. **What happens if I lose my Will?**
Ideally, you should make a new Will. If you are able to find a copy of your Will, you should seek the advice of a lawyer as to whether the copy can be used.

19. **Is my Will recognised worldwide?**
Yes, it is.

20. **Can my Will be challenged?**
Anyone can challenge a Will. The important issue is whether a challenge can be justified. You should seek the advice of a lawyer if you have concerns about challenges to your Will.

21. **Is there inheritance tax in Singapore?**
No, inheritance tax or estate duty was abolished on 15 February 2008.

22. **Will my beneficiaries incur property tax?**
Property tax is not imposed on beneficiaries if their share in the property is in accordance with a Will or intestacy rules, or Muslim *Faraidh* laws of inheritance. Property tax will be imposed in some cases where beneficiaries give or sell their shares to another.

You should seek the advice of a lawyer if you have concerns.

23. **Can I limit the powers of my trustee?**

    Yes, you can. More importantly, you can specify what type of powers your trustee should have.

24. **Do I need to declare all the information about my assets in my Will?**

    This depends on how you wish to distribute your assets.

25. **How do I alter my Will if my wishes change?**

    Ideally, you should do a new Will if you decide to change any of your wishes or instructions in the Will.

26. **Will it be cheaper to amend an existing Will?**

    This depends on the type of amendment, so you should check with your lawyer.

27. **We plan to have children in the future. Can we cover this in our Wills now?**

    It is best to update your Will once there is a significant change in your family situation. In this case, you may also want to update your Will so that you can appoint a person to be the guardian of your child.

28. **My partner and I are unmarried, and we are buying a property together, but I am contributing all of the deposit. Can this be recorded anywhere in the Will?**

    The primary function of a Will is to appoint an executor and beneficiaries. You should consult a lawyer as to the type of document that is most suitable to protect your interest for this arrangement to purchase a property.

29. Can my beneficiaries be foreigners or permanent residents (PRs)? Can they inherit my properties in Singapore?

Yes, they can. What they inherit will be subject to the prevailing property rules, such as the Residential Property Act, the HDB rules, etc.

30. Who will handle my instructions in the Will after I die?

Your executor, as appointed in your Will.

31. Must I list down all my bank account numbers, CDP and broker account numbers in my Will?

It depends on how you wish to distribute your assets.

32. Can I draft a Will myself?

The law does not prevent you from drafting your own Will. However, it is advisable to seek legal advice to address any concerns you may have and to help with any lack of understanding of the law.

33. How do I withdraw money and close a bank account with a Will?

Such matters are subject to the relevant terms and conditions set out by the bank for your account and also to the prevailing banking rules. Note that a Will is primarily a lawful way to appoint the executor and beneficiaries for an estate, and a bank would usually require the court order known as the Grant of Probate before the bank is satisfied that it may take instructions from the authorised representative of the estate.

34. Who can I appoint as an executor in my Will?

Appoint a person you trust to carry out your wishes

and who is able and willing to do so. For practical purposes, the person should not be too old.

35. Can my lawyer be the executor of my Will?

Yes, your lawyer is permitted to be your executor. It is best to check with your lawyer if he/she is prepared to do so and to check the fees for such a service.

36. How do I revoke my Will?

You can revoke your Will by making a new one or by destroying your current one.

37. Who should be the witness of my Will?

The witnesses for your Will are usually provided when you engage the services of a lawyer. Note that the witnesses for a Will should not be the beneficiaries of the Will.

38. Will my Will be affected if I legally change my name?

It is best to make a new Will to update it with your new name. Your name in your Will should be consistent with your legal name in your NRIC or passport, so that the application for the Grant of Probate will be a smooth process.

39. Can I make my Will online?

Yes, you can. However, do note that you will not have the benefit of legal advice in doing so.

40. What is required for my Will to be valid?

You have to comply with the formalities set out in sections 4, 5 and 6 of the Wills Act. See Chapter 3, under "How to Make a Valid Will".

41. Can my Will be a verbal recording?

No, it cannot be in the form of a verbal recording.

42. What if I die without writing a Will?

The rules of intestacy will apply if you die without a Will and the court will appoint an administrator to manage your estate and distribute your assets according to the rules.

43. Will my liabilities be transferred to my offspring upon my death?

Your liabilities and debts will come under your estate and your administrator (or executor if you have made a valid Will) will be responsible to pay them on behalf of your estate.

44. Do the beneficiaries of my Will have to be Singaporean?

Not necessarily, but some assets like immovable property are subject to rules about foreign ownership, such as HDB and landed property.

45. Can I transfer the ownership of my business through my Will?

If you have shares in a private limited company, you can give your shares under your Will. If you are an owner of a business, for example, a sole proprietor or partner, you may be able to give the assets of the business under your Will and you should seek the advice of a lawyer.

46. Does a person need to have a mental capacity assessment before writing a Will if they have dementia?

Yes, this is to ensure that a person has the necessary testamentary capacity before he/she can make a valid Will, as there are various stages of dementia and having a bad memory may not necessarily mean the person does not have the mental capacity to make a Will.

47. Does the Wills Registry keep a copy of my Will?

a. No, the registry keeps a record of information about your Will, but it does not keep a copy of your Will as it is not a depository. The Wills Registry is a confidential registry where people making a Will (or their lawyers) can deposit information on the Wills, and it is maintained by the Public Trustee.

b. One common misconception that many people have about registering their Wills at the Wills Registry is that the Wills Registry keeps actual copies of Wills. The Wills Registry keeps neither actual Wills nor photocopies. Rather, the Wills Registry keeps important information regarding Wills, such as:

    i. details of the person making the Will;

    ii. date of the Will;

    iii. details of the person who drew up the Will; and

    iv. details of where the Will is held.

c. Registration at the Wills Registry is not mandatory, and it does not have any impact on the validity of a Will. In addition, information held by the Wills Registry is strictly confidential, and only the following people have access to this information:

    i. the person who made the Will or his legal representative;

    ii. the lawyer acting for the deceased's estate;

    iii. the deceased's next of kin;

iv. the donee of a Lasting Power of Attorney (LPA) or a deputy appointed by the court, with powers to manage the testator's property and financial affairs if the testator lacks mental capacity; and

v. a person whom the Public Trustee considers to have a legitimate interest in the testator's will or estate.

48. Can I leave instructions regarding my pet(s) in my Will?

Yes, but you cannot leave money directly to an animal. You should therefore seek advice about setting up a trust for your pet(s).

49. I am not married to my partner but we have been together for a few years – what will happen to her/him when I die?

It does not matter how long you have been in a relationship with your partner. If you and your partner are not married when you die, she/he will not be entitled to any of your assets, unless you make a Will appointing your partner as a beneficiary. The same applies for stepchildren who are not legally adopted and illegitimate children. See Chapter 5, under "No Distribution Plan".

50. Can I exclude someone from my Will?

You are entitled to exclude anyone from your Will. However, take note that the law makes provision for a special class of persons under the Inheritance (Family Provision) Act. See Chapter 7, under "Claim for Reasonable Financial Provision against Estate".

CONCLUDING REMARKS

The purpose of this book is to help readers understand the whys and whats of making a Will. I would also urge readers to bear a few points in mind when embarking on making their Will.

Firstly, a Will is a worthwhile investment of time, effort and expense. Most people spend a significant amount of money on holidays and mobile devices over the course of their lives. However, it is common for many to have a small budget for their Will and cut corners on this crucial document thereby limiting its scope, by relying on the so-called "simple" or "no frills" Will. This is not in your best interests. Few would ignore a doctor's advice when it comes to medical treatment or simply choose the most basic or cheapest medication or therapy. Likewise, I urge you to seek and heed sound legal advice to make a Will that is most appropriate for your own personal circumstances.

Secondly, this book focuses on the whys and whats but not the how of making a Will. This was not included as, in my opinion, it should be left to a professional such as a lawyer who has the expertise to prepare your Will and advise you on your options after carefully listening to you about your situation and concerns. It should be tailored to your needs as each person's family situation is different and with different requirements. Just as you would not self-diagnose or self-treat a serious medical condition based only on information from an online search, I urge you to look to a professional instead of what you read on the Internet or use a pre-set template that may not serve you well or provide for your particular situation.

Thirdly, a Will is a great way to show your love for your family, in the form of the last words they will read from you. So let love be your motivation to make or update your Will, so that your loved ones are not inconvenienced or prejudiced when you are no longer with them.

> Love is patient and kind; love does not envy or boast; it is not
> arrogant or rude.
> It does not insist on its own way; it is not irritable or
> resentful; it does not rejoice
> at wrongdoing, but rejoices with the truth. Love bears all
> things,
> believes all things, hopes all things, endures all things.
>
> **1 Corinthians 13**

Do not unintentionally cause more grief for your loved ones when they survive you by not making a comprehensive Will for them. Remember, you are doing it for them, not yourself!

ANNEX

Wills Act (Cap 352, 1996 Rev Ed)

Intestate Succession Act (Cap 146, 2013 Rev Ed)

Inheritance (Family Provision) Act (Cap 138, 1985 Rev Ed)

Probate and Administration Act (Cap 251, 2000 Rev Ed) – Extracts

Legitimacy Act (Cap 162, 1985 Rev Ed)

WILLS ACT
(CHAPTER 352)
(Original Enactment: Indian Act XXV of 1838)
REVISED EDITION 1996
(27th December 1996)

An Act to declare the law relating to wills.

[8th October 1838]

Short title

1. This Act may be cited as the Wills Act.

Interpretation

2. In this Act, unless the context otherwise requires —

"internal law", in relation to any territory or state, means the law which would apply in a case where no question of the law in force in any other territory or state arose;

"personal estate" shall extend to leasehold estates and other chattels real, and also to moneys, shares of Government and other funds, securities for money, not being real estates, debts, choses in action, rights, credits, goods and all other property whatsoever which by law devolves upon the executor or administrator, and to any share or interest therein;

"real estate" shall extend to messuages, lands, rents and hereditaments, whether corporeal, incorporeal or personal, and to any undivided share thereof and to any estate, right or interest, other than a chattel interest, therein;

"state" means a territory or group of territories having its own law of nationality;

"will" includes a testament and an appointment by will or by writing in the nature of a will in exercise of a power and also a disposition by will and testament and any other testamentary disposition.

[24/92]

[7/97 wef 01/10/1997]

Property disposable by will

3.—(1) Subject to the provisions of this Act, every person may devise, bequeath or dispose of by his will, executed in the manner required under this Act, all real estate and all personal estate which he shall be entitled to either at law or in equity at the time of his death.

(2) The power given under subsection (1) shall extend to —

(a) all estates pur autre vie, whether there shall or shall not be any special occupant thereof, whether the same shall be a corporeal or an incorporeal hereditament, and whether the same shall be freehold or of any other tenure;

(b) all contingent, executory or other future interests in any real or personal estate, whether the testator may or may not be ascertained as the person or one of the persons in whom the same respectively may become vested, and whether he may be entitled thereto under the instrument by which the same respectively were created or under any disposition thereof by deed or will;

(c) all rights of entry for conditions broken and other rights of entry; and

(d) such of the same estates, interests and rights respectively and other real and personal estates as the testator may be entitled to at the time of his death notwithstanding that he may become entitled to the same subsequently to the execution of his will.

Will of infant invalid

4. No will made by any person under the age of 21 years shall be valid.

Rules as to formal validity

5.—(1) This section shall take effect notwithstanding any other provisions of this Act.

[24/92]

(2) A will shall be treated as properly executed if its execution conformed to the internal law in force —

(a) in the territory where it was executed;

(b) in the territory where the testator was domiciled at the time —

(i) when the will was executed; or

(ii) of his death;

138

(c) in the territory where the testator habitually resided at either of the times referred to in paragraph (b); or

(d) in the state of which the testator was a national at either of the times referred to in paragraph (b).

[24/92]

(3) Without prejudice to subsection (2), the following shall be treated as properly executed:

(a) a will executed on board a vessel or an aircraft of any description, if the execution of the will conformed to the internal law in force in the territory with which, having regard to its registration (if any) and other relevant circumstances, the vessel or aircraft may be taken to have been most closely connected;

(b) a will so far as it disposes of immovable property, if its execution conformed to the internal law in force in the territory where the property was situated;

(c) a will so far as it revokes a will which under this Act would be treated as properly executed or revokes a provision which under this Act would be treated as comprised in a properly executed will, if the execution of the later will conformed to any law by reference to which the revoked will or provision would be treated as properly executed;

(d) a will so far as it exercises a power of appointment, if the execution of the will conformed to the law governing the essential validity of the power.

[24/92]

(4) A will so far as it exercises a power of appointment shall not be treated as improperly executed by reason only that its execution was not in accordance with any formal requirements contained in the instrument creating the power.

[24/92]

(5) In determining for the purposes of this section whether or not the execution of a will conformed to a particular law, regard shall be had to the formal requirements of that law at the time of execution, but this shall not prevent account being taken of an alteration of law affecting wills executed at that time if the alteration enables the will to be treated as properly executed.

[24/92]

(6) Where a law in force outside Singapore falls to be applied in relation to a will, any requirement of that law whereby special formalities are to be observed by testators answering a particular description, or witnesses to the execution of a will are to possess certain qualifications, shall be treated, notwithstanding any rule of that law to the contrary, as a formal requirement only.

[24/92]

(7) The construction of a will shall not be altered by reason of any change in the testator's domicile after the execution of the will.

[24/92]

(8) Where under this section the internal law in force in any territory or state is to be applied in the case of a will, but there are in force in that territory or state two or more systems of internal law relating to the formal validity of wills, the system to be applied shall be ascertained as follows:

(a) if there is in force throughout the territory or state a rule indicating which of those systems can properly be applied in the case in question, that rule shall be followed; or

(b) if there is no such rule, the system shall be that with which the testator was most closely connected at the relevant time, and for this purpose the relevant time is the time of the testator's death where the matter is to be determined by reference to circumstances prevailing at his death, and the time of execution of the will in any other case.

[24/92]

(9) This section shall not apply to a will of a testator who died before 26th June 1992 and shall apply to a will of a testator who dies after that date whether the will was executed before or after that date.

[4A

[24/92]

Mode of execution

6.—(1) No will shall be valid unless it is in writing and executed in the manner mentioned in subsection (2).

(2) Every will shall be signed at the foot or end thereof by the testator, or by some other person in his presence and by his direction, and the signature shall be made or acknowledged by the testator

as the signature to his will or codicil in the presence of two or more witnesses present at the same time, and those witnesses shall subscribe the will in the presence of the testator, but no form of attestation shall be necessary.

(3) Every will shall, as far only as regards the position of the signature of the testator, or of the person signing for him as mentioned in subsection (2), be deemed to be valid under this section if the signature shall be so placed at or after, or following, or under, or beside, or opposite to the end of the will, that it shall be apparent on the face of the will that the testator intended to give effect by such his signature to the writing signed as his will; and no such will shall be affected by the circumstance —

(a) that the signature shall not follow or be immediately after the foot or end of the will;

(b) that a blank space shall intervene between the concluding word of the will and the signature;

(c) that the signature shall be placed among the words of the testimonium clause or of the clause of attestation, or shall follow or be after or under the clause of attestation, either with or without a blank space intervening, or shall follow or be after, or under, or beside the names or one of the names of the subscribing witnesses;

(d) that the signature shall be on a side or page or other portion of the paper or papers containing the will whereon no clause or paragraph or disposing part of the will shall be written above the signature; or

(e) that there shall appear to be sufficient space on or at the bottom of the preceding side or page or other portion of the same paper on which the will is written to contain the signature.

[21/38]

(4) The enumeration of the circumstances under subsection (3) shall not restrict the generality of that subsection; but no signature under this Act shall be operative to give effect to any disposition or direction which is underneath or which follows it, nor shall it give effect to any disposition or direction inserted after the signature shall be made.

[5

Execution of appointment by will

7.—(1) No appointment made by will, in exercise of any power, shall be valid, unless the will is executed in the manner required by this Act.

(2) Every will executed in the manner required by this Act shall, so far as respects the execution and attestation thereof, be a valid execution of a power of appointment by will, notwithstanding that it shall have been expressly required that a will made in exercise of that power should be executed with some additional or other form of execution or solemnity.

[6

Publication of will not necessary

8. Every will executed in the manner required by this Act shall be valid without any other publication thereof.

[7

Will not to be invalidated by reason of incompetency of attesting witness

9. If any person who attests the execution of a will shall, at the time of the execution thereof or at any time afterwards, be incompetent to be admitted a witness to prove the execution thereof, the will shall not on that account be invalid.

[8

Gifts to attesting witness or to wife or husband of attesting witness to be void

10.—(1) If any person attests the execution of any will to whom or to whose wife or husband any beneficial devise, legacy, estate, interest, gift or appointment of or affecting any real or personal estate, other than and except charges and directions for the payment of any debt, shall be thereby given or made, the devise, legacy, estate, interest, gift or appointment shall, so far only as concerns the person attesting the execution of the will, or the wife or husband of that person, or any person claiming under that person or wife or husband, be utterly null and void.

[24/92]

(2) The attesting witness referred to in subsection (1) shall be admitted as a witness to prove the execution of the will or to prove the validity or invalidity thereof, notwithstanding the devise, legacy, estate, interest, gift or appointment mentioned in the will.

(3) The attestation of a will by a person to whom or to whose spouse there is given or made any disposition as is described in subsection (1) shall be disregarded for the purposes of that subsection if the will is duly executed without his attestation and without that of any other such person.

[24/92]

(4) Subsection (3) shall apply to the will of any person dying after the passing of the Wills (Amendment) Act 1992, whether executed before or after the passing of that Act.

[9

[24/92]

Creditor attesting a will charging estate with debts to be admitted a witness

11. In case by any will any real or personal estate shall be charged with any debt, and any creditor, or the wife or husband of any creditor, whose debt is so charged, shall attest the execution of the will, the creditor notwithstanding the charge shall be admitted a witness to prove the execution of the will or to prove the validity or invalidity thereof.

[10

Executor not incompetent to be witness

12. No person shall, on account of his being an executor of a will, be incompetent to be admitted a witness to prove the execution of the will or to prove the validity or invalidity thereof.

[11

Will to be revoked by marriage except in certain cases

13.—(1) Every will made by a man or woman shall be revoked by his or her marriage, except a will made in exercise of a power of appointment, when the real or personal estate thereby appointed would not in default of such appointment pass to his or her heir, executor or administrator or the person entitled under the ISA.

(2) Notwithstanding subsection (1), where a will made on or after 29th August 1938 is expressed to be made in contemplation of a marriage, the will shall not be revoked by the solemnization of the marriage contemplated; and this subsection shall apply notwithstanding that the marriage contemplated may be the first, second or subsequent marriage of a person lawfully practising polygamy.

[12

[21/38]

No will to be revoked by presumption from altered circumstances

14. No will shall be revoked by any presumption of an intention on the ground of an alteration in circumstances.

[13

Revocation of will or codicil

15. No will or codicil, or any part thereof, shall be revoked otherwise than —

(a) as provided in section 13;

(b) by another will or codicil executed in the manner by this Act required;

(c) by some writing declaring an intention to revoke it, and executed in the manner in which a will is by this Act required to be executed; or

(d) by the burning, tearing, or otherwise destroying the will by the testator, or by some person in his presence and by his direction, with the intention of revoking it.

[14

Effect of obliteration, interlineation or alteration

16.—(1) No obliteration, interlineation or other alteration made in any will after the execution thereof shall be valid or have any effect except so far as the words or effect of the will before such alteration shall not be apparent, unless the alteration shall be executed in the like manner as by this Act is required for the execution of the will.

[22/49]

(2) A will referred to in subsection (1), with such alteration as part thereof, shall be deemed to be duly executed if the signature of the testator and the subscription of the witnesses be made in the margin or on some other part of the will opposite or near to the alteration or at the foot or end of or opposite to a memorandum referring to the alteration and written at the end or some other part of the will.

[15

Revival of revoked will

17.—(1) No will or codicil, or any part thereof, which shall be in any manner revoked, shall be revived otherwise than by the re-execution thereof, or by a codicil executed in the manner required by this Act and showing an intention to revive the will or codicil.

(2) When any will or codicil which shall be partly revoked, and afterwards wholly revoked, shall be revived, the revival shall not extend to so much thereof as shall have been revoked before the revocation of the whole thereof, unless an intention to the contrary be shown.

[16

Subsequent conveyance or other acts not to prevent operation of will

18. No conveyance or other act made or done subsequently to the execution of a will of or relating to any real or personal estate therein comprised, except an act by which the will shall be revoked as aforesaid, shall prevent the operation of the will with respect to the estate or interest in the real or personal estate as the testator shall have power to dispose of by will at the time of his death.

[17

Will to be construed to speak from death of testator

19. Every will shall be construed with reference to the real estate and personal estate comprised in it, to speak and take effect as if it had been executed immediately before the death of the testator, unless a contrary intention shall appear by the will.

[18

Residuary devises to include estates comprised in lapsed and void devises

20. Unless a contrary intention appears by the will, such real estate

and interest therein as is comprised or intended to be comprised in any devise in the will contained, which fails or is void by reason of the death of the devisee in the lifetime of the testator or by reason of the devise being contrary to law or otherwise incapable of taking effect, shall be included in the residuary devise (if any) contained in the will.

[19

General gift of realty and of personality to include property over which testator has general power of appointment

21.—(1) A general devise of the real estate of the testator, or of the real estate of the testator in any place or in the occupation of any person mentioned in his will, or otherwise described in a general manner, shall be construed to include any real estate, or any real estate to which that description shall extend, as the case may be, which he may have power to appoint in any manner he may think proper, and shall operate as an execution of that power, unless a contrary intention shall appear by the will.

(2) A bequest of the personal estate of the testator, or any bequest of personal estate described in a general manner, shall be construed to include any personal estate, or any personal estate to which that description shall extend, as the case may be, which he may have power to appoint in any manner he may think proper, and shall operate as an execution of that power, unless a contrary intention shall appear by the will.

[20

Devise without words of limitation

22. Where any real estate shall be devised to any person without any words of limitation, the devise shall be construed to pass the fee simple or other the whole estate or interest which the testator had power to dispose of by will in the real estate unless a contrary intention shall appear by the will.

[21

Construction of words importing want or failure of issue

23.—(1) In any devise or bequest of real or personal estate, the words "die without issue" or "die without leaving issue", or any other words which may import either a want or failure of issue of any person in his lifetime or at the time of his death, or an indefinite failure of his issue, shall be construed to mean a want or failure of issue in the lifetime or at the time of the death of that person, and not an indefinite failure of his issue, unless a contrary intention shall appear by the will.

(2) This Act shall not extend to cases where those words referred to in subsection (1) import if no issue described in a preceding gift shall be born, or if there shall be no issue who shall live to attain the age or otherwise answer the description required for obtaining a vested estate by a preceding gift to such issue.

[22

Devise of real estate to trustee or executor

24. Where any real estate shall be devised to any trustee or executor, the devise shall be construed to pass the fee simple or other the whole estate or interest which the testator had power to dispose of by will in the real estate, unless a definite term of years, absolute or determinable, or an estate of freehold, shall thereby be given to him expressly or by implication.

[23

Devise of real estate to trustee without limitation

25. Where any real estate shall be devised to a trustee, without any express limitation of the estate to be taken by the trustee, and the beneficial interest in such real estate, or in the surplus rents and profits thereof, shall not be given to any person for life, or the beneficial interest shall be given to any person for life, but the purposes of the trust may continue beyond the life of that person, the devise shall be construed to vest in the trustee the fee simple, or other the whole legal estate which the testator had power to dispose of by will in the real estate, and not an estate determinable when the purposes of the trust shall be satisfied.

[24

Gifts to children or other issue who leave issue living at testator's death not to lapse

26. Where any person being a child or other issue of the testator to whom any real or personal estate shall be devised or bequeathed for any estate or interest not determinable at or before the death of that person shall die in the lifetime of the testator leaving issue, and any such issue of that person shall be living at the time of the death of the testator, that devise or bequest shall not lapse, but shall take effect as if

the death of that person had happened immediately after the death of the testator, unless a contrary intention shall appear by the will.

[25

Saving as to wills of soldiers and mariners

27.—(1) Notwithstanding anything in this Act, any soldier being in actual military service, or any mariner or seaman being at sea, may dispose of his personal estate as he might have done before the making of this Act and may do so even though under the age of 21 years.

[21/38]

Validity of testamentary dispositions of real property made by soldiers and sailors

(2) A testamentary disposition of any real estate made by a person to whom this section applies, and who dies after 29th August 1938 shall, notwithstanding that the person making the disposition was at the time of making it under 21 years of age or that the disposition has not been made in such manner or form as was on 29th August 1938 required by law, be valid in any case where the person making the disposition was of such age and the disposition has been made in such manner and form that if the disposition had been a disposition of personal estate made by that person it would have been valid.

[21/38]

Power to appoint testamentary guardians

(3) Where any person dies after 29th August 1938 having made a will which is, or which, if it had been a disposition of property, would have been rendered valid by this section, any appointment contained in that will of any person as guardian of the infant children of the testator shall be of full force and effect.

[21/38]

Section to extend to naval, marine and air forces

(4) This section shall extend to any member of any naval or marine forces not only when he is at sea but also when he is so circumstanced that if he were a soldier he would be in actual military service within the meaning of this section.

[21/38]

(5) For the purposes of this section, "soldier" includes a member of an air force.

[26

[21/38]

Rectification of will

28.—(1) A court may order that a will be rectified so as to carry out the testator's intentions, if the court is satisfied that, as a consequence of either or both of the following, the will is so expressed that the will fails to carry out the testator's intentions:

  (a) a clerical error;

  (b) a failure to understand the testator's instructions.

(2) Except with the permission of a court, an application for an order under subsection (1) must be made no later than 6 months after the date on which a grant authorising the administration of the testator's estate is first made.

(3) Where the personal representatives of the testator distribute, after the end of the period of 6 months referred to in subsection (2), any part of the testator's estate —

  (a) this section does not render the personal representatives liable for making that distribution on the ground that they ought to have taken into account the possibility that a court may permit the making of an application for an order under subsection (1) after the end of that period; but

  (b) this subsection does not affect any power to recover, by reason of the making of an order under subsection (1), any part of the testator's estate that is so distributed.

(4) The following grants are to be disregarded when considering, for the purposes of this section, when a grant authorising the administration of the testator's estate is first made:

  (a) a grant limited to settled land or to trust property;

  (b) any other grant that does not permit the distribution of the testator's estate;

  (c) a grant limited to a part only of the testator's estate, unless a grant limited to the remainder of the testator's estate has previously been made or is made at the same time.

(5) For the purposes of this section, where a grant consists of any probate, or letters of administration with the will annexed, sealed under section 47(1) of the Probate and Administration Act (Cap. 251), the grant is deemed to be made on the date of sealing of the probate or letters of administration with the will annexed.

(6) The Family Justice Rules Committee constituted under section 46(1) of the Family Justice Act 2014 (Act 27 of 2014) may make Family Justice Rules —

  (a) to regulate and prescribe the procedure and practice to be followed in any application for an order under subsection (1); and

  (b) to provide for any matter relating to any such procedure or practice.

(7) In this section —

"court" means the High Court or a Family Court;

"grant" means any of the following:

  (a) any probate granted by the High Court or a Family Court, or granted before 1 January 2015 by a District Court;

  (b) any letters of administration with the will annexed granted by the High Court or a Family Court, or granted before 1 January 2015 by a District Court;

  (c) any probate, or letters of administration with the will annexed, sealed under section 47(1) of the Probate and Administration Act;

"letters of administration with the will annexed" and "probate" have the same meanings as in section 2 of the Probate and Administration Act.

[Act 16 of 2016 wef 01/12/2016]

INTESTATE SUCCESSION ACT
(CHAPTER 146)
(Original Enactment: Act 7 of 1967)
REVISED EDITION 2013
(31st December 2013)

An Act to make provision for the distribution of intestate estates.

[2nd June 1967]

Short title

1. This Act may be cited as the Intestate Succession Act.

Application

2. Nothing in this Act shall apply to the estate of any Muslim or shall affect any rules of the Muslim law in respect of the distribution of the estate of any such person.

Interpretation

3. In this Act —

"child" means a legitimate child and includes any child adopted by virtue of an order of court under any written law for the time being in force in Singapore, Malaysia or Brunei Darussalam;

"intestate" includes any person who leaves a will but dies intestate as to some beneficial interest in his property;

"issue" includes children and the descendants of deceased children.

Law regulating distribution

4.—(1) The distribution of the movable property of a person deceased shall be regulated by the law of the country in which he was domiciled at the time of his death.

(2) The distribution of the immovable property of a person deceased shall be regulated by this Act wherever he may have been domiciled at the time of his death.

Property of intestate to be distributed

5. If a person dies intestate after 2nd June 1967, he being at the time of his death —

(a) domiciled in Singapore and possessed beneficially of property, whether movable or immovable, or both, situated in Singapore; or

(b) domiciled outside Singapore and possessed beneficially of immovable property situated in Singapore,
that property or the proceeds thereof, after payment thereout of the expenses of due administration as prescribed by the Probate and Administration Act (Cap. 251), shall be distributed among the persons entitled to succeed beneficially to that property or the proceeds thereof.

Persons held to be similarly related to deceased

6. For the purposes of distribution —

(a) there shall be no distinction between those who are related to a person deceased through his father and those who are related to him through his mother nor between those who were actually born in his lifetime and those who at the date of his death were only conceived in the womb but who have subsequently been born alive; and

(b) those related to a person deceased by the half blood shall rank immediately after those of the whole blood related to him in the same degree.

Rules for distribution

7. In effecting such distribution, the following rules shall be observed:

Rule 1

If an intestate dies leaving a surviving spouse, no issue and no parent, the spouse shall be entitled to the whole of the estate.

Rule 2

If an intestate dies leaving a surviving spouse and issue, the spouse shall be entitled to one-half of the estate.

Rule 3

Subject to the rights of the surviving spouse, if any, the estate (both as to the undistributed portion and the reversionary interest) of an intestate who leaves issue shall be distributed by equal portions per stirpes to and amongst the children of the person dying intestate and such persons as legally represent those children, in case any of those children be then dead.

Proviso No. (1) — The persons who legally represent the children of an intestate are their descendants and not their next of kin.

Proviso No. (2) — Descendants of the intestate to the remotest degree stand in the place of their parent or other ancestor, and take according to their stocks the share which he or she would have taken.

Rule 4

If an intestate dies leaving a surviving spouse and no issue but a parent or parents, the spouse shall be entitled to one-half of the estate and the parent or parents to the other half of the estate.

Rule 5

If there are no descendants, the parent or parents of the intestate shall take the estate, in equal portions if there be 2 parents, subject to the rights of the surviving spouse (if any) as provided in rule 4.

Rule 6

If there are no surviving spouse, descendants or parents, the brothers and sisters and children of deceased brothers or sisters of the intestate shall share the estate in equal portions between the brothers and sisters and the children of any deceased brother or sister shall take according to their stocks the share which the deceased brother or sister would have taken.

Rule 7

If there are no surviving spouse, descendants, parents, brothers and sisters or children of such brothers and sisters but grandparents of the intestate, the grandparents shall take the whole of the estate in equal portions.

Rule 8

If there are no surviving spouse, descendants, parents, brothers and sisters or their children or grandparents but uncles and aunts of the intestate, the uncles and aunts shall take the whole of the estate in equal portions.

Rule 9

In default of distribution under rules 1 to 8, the Government shall be entitled to the whole of the estate.

Special provision if intestate leaves lawful widows

8. If any person so dying intestate leaves surviving him more than one wife, such wives shall share among them equally the share that the wife of the intestate would have been entitled to, had the intestate left only one wife surviving him.

Children's advancement not to be taken into account

9. Where a distributive share of the property of a person dying intestate is claimed by a child or any descendant of a child of that person, no money or other property which the intestate may during his life have given, paid or settled to or for the advancement of the child by whom or by whose descendant the claim is made shall be taken into account in estimating such distributive share.

Application to cases of partial intestacy

10. Where any person dies leaving a will beneficially disposing of part of his property, the provisions of this Act shall have effect as respects the part of his property not so disposed of, subject to the provisions contained in the will:

Provided that the personal representative shall, subject to his rights and powers for the purposes of administration, be a trustee for the persons entitled under this Act in respect of the part of the estate not expressly disposed of unless it appears by the will that the personal representative is entitled to take that part beneficially.

INHERITANCE (FAMILY PROVISION) ACT
(CHAPTER 138)
(Original Enactment: Act 28 of 1966)
REVISED EDITION 1985
(30th March 1987)

An Act relating to the disposition of estates of deceased persons and for other purposes connected therewith.

[16th September 1966]

Short title and application

1.—(1) This Act may be cited as the Inheritance (Family Provision) Act.

(2) This Act shall not apply to the estates of deceased Muslims.

Interpretation

2. In this Act, unless the context otherwise requires —

"annual income" means, in relation to the net estate of a deceased person, the income that the net estate might be expected at the date of the order made under this Act, when realised, to yield in a year;

"court" means the High Court or a Family Court;

[Act 27 of 2014 wef 01/10/2014]

"death duties" means estate duty and every other duty leviable or payable on death;

"net estate" means all the property of which a deceased person had power to dispose by his will (otherwise than by virtue of a special power of appointment) less the amount of his funeral, testamentary and administration expenses, debts and liabilities and estate duty payable out of his estate on his death;

"Registrar" means the registrar of the Family Justice Courts;

[Act 27 of 2014 wef 01/10/2014]

"will" includes any codicil or other testamentary document;

"son" and "daughter", respectively, include a male or female child adopted by the deceased by virtue of an order made under the provisions of any written law relating to the adoption of children for the time being in force in Singapore, Malaysia or Brunei Darussalam, and also the son or daughter of the deceased en ventre sa mere at the date of the death of the deceased.

Power for court to order payment out of net estate of deceased for benefit of surviving spouse or child

3.—(1) Where, after the commencement of this Act, a person dies domiciled in Singapore leaving —

(a) a wife or husband;

(b) a daughter who has not been married or who is, by reason of some mental or physical disability, incapable of maintaining herself;

(c) an infant son; or

(d) a son who is, by reason of some mental or physical disability, incapable of maintaining himself,

then, if the court on application by or on behalf of any such wife, husband, daughter or son as aforesaid (referred to in this Act as a dependant of the deceased) is of opinion that the disposition of the deceased's estate effected by his will, or the law relating to intestacy, or the combination of his will and that law, is not such as to make reasonable provision for the maintenance of that dependant, the court may order that such reasonable provision as the court thinks fit shall, subject to such conditions or restrictions, if any, as the court may impose, be made out of the deceased's net estate for the maintenance of that dependant:

Provided that no application shall be made to the court by or on behalf of any person in any case where the disposition of a deceased's estate effected as aforesaid is such that the surviving spouse is entitled to not less than two-thirds of the income of the net estate and where the only other dependant or dependants, if any, is or are a child or children of the surviving spouse.

(2) The provision for maintenance to be made by an order shall, subject to subsection (4), be by way of periodical payments and the order shall provide for their termination not later than —

(a) in the case of a wife or husband, her or his remarriage;

(b) in the case of a daughter who has not been married, or who is under disability, her marriage or the cesser of her disability, whichever is the later;

- (c) in the case of an infant son, his attaining the age of 21 years;
- (d) in the case of a son under disability, the cesser of his disability, or in any case, his or her earlier death.

(3) Periodical payments made under subsection (2) to any one dependant shall not be at an annual rate which exceeds the annual income of the net estate, and, where payments are so made to more than one dependant in respect of the same period, the aggregate of the annual rates at which those payments are made shall not exceed the annual income of the net estate.

(4) Where the value of a deceased's net estate does not exceed $50,000, the court shall have power to make an order providing for maintenance, in whole or in part, by way of a lump sum payment.

(5) In determining whether, and in what way, and as from what date, provision for maintenance ought to be made by an order, the court shall have regard to the nature of the property representing the deceased's net estate and shall not order any such provision to be made as would necessitate a realisation that would be improvident having regard to the interests of the deceased's dependants and of the person who, apart from the order, would be entitled to that property.

(6) The court shall, on any application made under this Act, have regard to any past, present or future capital or income from any source of the dependant of the deceased to whom the application relates, to the conduct of that dependant in relation to the deceased and otherwise, and to any other matter or thing which in the circumstances of the case the court may consider relevant or material in relation to that dependant, to persons interested in the estate of the deceased, or otherwise.

(7) The court shall also, on any such application, have regard to the deceased's reasons, so far as ascertainable, for making the dispositions made by his will (if any), or for refraining from disposing by will of his estate or part of his estate, or for not making any provision, or any further provision, as the case may be, for a dependant, and the court may accept such evidence of those reasons as it considers sufficient including any statement in writing signed by the deceased and dated, so, however, that in estimating the weight, if any, to be attached to any such statement the court shall have regard to all the circumstances from which any inference can reasonably be drawn as to the accuracy or otherwise of the statement.

(8) The court in considering for the purposes of subsection (1), whether the disposition of the deceased's estate effected by the law relating to intestacy, or by the combination of the deceased's will and that law, makes reasonable provision for the maintenance of a dependant shall not be bound to assume that the law relating to intestacy makes reasonable provision in all cases.

Time within which application must be made

4.—(1) Except as provided by this section or section 6, an order under this Act shall not be made save on an application made within 6 months from the date on which representation in regard to the deceased's estate is first taken out.

(2) If it is shown to the satisfaction of the court that the limitation to the said period of 6 months would operate unfairly —

  (a) in consequence of the discovery of a will or codicil involving a substantial change in the disposition of the deceased's estate (whether or not involving a further grant of representation);

  (b) in consequence of a question whether a person had an interest in the estate; or as to the nature of an interest in the estate, not having been determined at the time when representation was first taken out; or

  (c) in consequence of some other circumstances affecting the administration or distribution of the estate, the court may extend that period.

(3) The provisions of this Act shall not render the personal representatives of the deceased liable for having distributed any part of the estate of the deceased after the expiration of the said period of 6 months on the ground that they ought to have taken into account the possibility that the court might exercise its power to extend that period, but this subsection shall be without prejudice to any power to recover any part of the estate so distributed arising by virtue of the making of an order under this Act.

(4) In considering under this section the question when representation was first taken out, a grant limited to trust property shall be left out of account unless a grant limited to the remainder of the estate has previously been made or is made at the same time.

(5) For the purposes of sections 18(2) and 38 of the Probate and Administration Act [Cap. 251] a dependant of a deceased person

by whom or on whose behalf an application made under this Act is proposed to be made shall be deemed to be a person interested in his estate.

Effect and form of order

5.—(1) Where an order is made under this Act, then for all purposes, including the purposes of the enactments relating to death duties, the will or the law relating to intestacy, or both the will and the law relating to intestacy, as the case may be, shall have effect, and shall be deemed to have had effect as from the deceased's death, subject to such variations as may be specified in the order for the purpose of giving effect to the provision for maintenance thereby made.

(2) The court may give such consequential directions as it thinks fit for the purpose of giving effect to an order made under this Act, but no larger part of the net estate shall be set aside or appropriated to answer by the income thereof the provision for maintenance thereby made than such a part as, at the date of the order, is sufficient to produce by the income thereof the amount of the said provision.

(3) An office copy of every order made under this Act shall be sent to the Registrar for entry and filing, and a memorandum of the order shall be endorsed on, or permanently annexed to, the probate or letters of administration under which the estate is being administered.

Variation of orders

6.—(1) On an application made at a date after the expiration of the period specified in section 4(1), or, as the case may be, of that period as extended under section 4(2), the court may make such an order as is hereinafter mentioned, but only as respects property the income of which is at that date applicable for the maintenance of a dependant of the deceased, that is to say —

(a) an order for varying the previous order on the ground that a material fact was not disclosed to the court when the order was made, or that a substantial change has taken place in the circumstances of the dependant or of a person beneficially interested in the property under the will or, as the case may be, under the law relating to intestacy; or

(b) an order for making provision for the maintenance of another dependant of the deceased.

(2) An application to the court for an order under subsection (1)(a) may be made by or on behalf of a dependant of the deceased or by the trustees of the property or by or on behalf of a person beneficially interested therein under the will or, as the case may be, under the law relating to intestacy.

The following is a reproduction of extracts only from the Probate and Administration Act. For the complete statute, please refer to Singapore Statutes Online.

PROBATE AND ADMINISTRATION ACT
(CHAPTER 251)
(Original Enactment: Ordinance 24 of 1934)
REVISED EDITION 2000
(1st July 2000)

An Act relating to the grant of probate and letters of administration.

[1st January 1935]

PART I

PRELIMINARY

Short title

1. This Act may be cited as the Probate and Administration Act.

Interpretation

2. In this Act, unless there is something repugnant in the subject or context —

"court" means the High Court or a Family Court;

[Act 27 of 2014 wef 01/01/2015]

[Deleted by Act 27 of 2014 wef 01/01/2015]

"letters of administration" means a grant under the seal of the court issuing the same, authorising the person or persons therein named to administer an intestate's estate in accordance with law;

"letters of administration with the will annexed" means a grant under the seal of the court issuing the same, authorising the person or persons therein named to administer a testator's estate in compliance with the directions contained in his will, and in accordance with law;

"prescribed form" means the form prescribed by rules made under any law for the time being in force relating to the courts;

"probate" means a grant under the seal of the court issuing the same, authorising the executor or executors expressly or impliedly appointed by a testator's will, or one or more of them, to administer the testator's estate in compliance with the directions contained in his will, and in accordance with law;

"probate action" means a cause or matter in which a probate application is contested by any person, and includes any application to alter or revoke the grant of any probate or letters of administration;

[42/2005 wef 01/01/2006]

"probate application" means an application for a grant of probate or letters of administration, and "probate applicant" shall be construed accordingly;

[42/2005 wef 01/01/2006]

"Public Trustee" means the Public Trustee appointed under the Public Trustee Act (Cap. 260) and includes a Deputy Public Trustee and an Assistant Public Trustee appointed under that Act;

[6/2004 wef 08/03/2004]

[Act 44 of 2014 wef 31/12/2014]

"registrar" means the registrar of the Family Justice Courts;

[Act 27 of 2014 wef 01/01/2015]

"will" includes any codicil or other testamentary document.

[7/97]

PART II

RENUNCIATION

Express renunciation

3.—(1) Any person who is or may become entitled to any probate or letters of administration may expressly renounce his right to such grant.

(2) Such renunciation may be made —

(a) orally by the person renouncing or by his advocate and solicitor, on the hearing of any probate application or probate action; or

[42/2005 wef 01/01/2006]

(b) in writing signed by the person so renouncing and attested either by an advocate and solicitor or by any person before whom an affidavit may be sworn.

Constructive renunciation

4.—(1) Any person having or claiming any interest in the estate of a deceased person, or any creditor of a deceased person, may, without applying for probate or letters of administration, cause to be issued a citation directed to the executor or executors appointed by the deceased's will, or to any person appearing to have a prior right to probate or letters of administration, calling upon the person cited to accept or renounce that right.

(2) Any person so cited may enter an appearance to the citation, but if he makes default in appearance thereto, he shall be deemed to have renounced his right.

(3) If, having appeared, the person so cited does not proceed to apply for probate or letters of administration, the person so citing may apply for an order that the person cited, unless he applies for and obtains a grant within a time limited by the order, shall be deemed to have renounced his right thereto, and an order may be made accordingly.

Effect of renunciation

5.—(1) The renunciation, whether made expressly in the manner provided by section 3, or constructively in the manner provided by section 4, shall preclude the person so renouncing from applying thereafter for probate or letters of administration.

(2) Notwithstanding subsection (1), the court may at any time allow the person so renouncing to withdraw his renunciation for the purpose of taking a grant, if it is shown that the withdrawal is for the benefit of the estate or of those interested under the will or intestacy.

PART III

GRANT OF PROBATE OR LETTERS OF ADMINISTRATION

Provisions as to number of personal representatives

6.—(1) Probate or letters of administration shall not be granted to more than 4 persons in respect of the same property.

(2) Letters of administration shall, if there is a minority or if a life inteest arises under the will, be granted either to a trust corporation, with or without an individual, or to not less than 2 individuals.

(3) The court in granting letters of administration may act on such prima facie evidence, furnished by the applicant or any other person, as to whether or not there is a minority or life interest, as may be prescribed by rules made under any written law for the time being in force relating to the courts.

(4) If there is only one personal representative (not being a trust corporation) then, during the minority of a beneficiary or the subsistence of a life interest and until the estate is fully administered, the court may, on the application of any person interested or of the guardian, committee or receiver of any such person, appoint one or more personal representatives in addition to the existing personal representative in accordance with rules made under any written law for the time being in force relating to the courts.

(5) This section shall apply to grants made after 1st January 1935 whether the testator or intestate died before or after that date.

(6) For the purposes of this section, "trust corporation" means the Public Trustee or a corporation licensed as a trust company under the Trust Companies Act 2005.

[11/2005 wef 01/02/2006]

Notation of domicile

7.—(1) A probate applicant may at any time apply to the registrar by summons intituled in the estate of the deceased person for an order that a notation be endorsed on the grant that the deceased person died domiciled in Singapore.

[42/2005 wef 01/01/2006]

(2) The registrar, on being satisfied by affidavit and by such further evidence as he may require that the testator or intestate died domiciled in Singapore, may write and sign a note or memorandum upon such grant stating that the testator or intestate died domiciled in Singapore.

Grant of probate

8.—(1) Probate may be granted to any executor appointed by a will.

(2) The appointment may be express or implied.

(3) Subject to section 6, where more than one person is appointed an executor by a will, probate may be granted to one or more of the persons so appointed, without prejudice to a subsequent application by another or others of them for further grant or grants.

Where will lost, etc.

Probate of copy or draft, or of contents

9. Where a will has been lost or mislaid after the death of the testator, or where a will cannot for any sufficient reason be produced —

   (a) if a copy or draft thereof is produced, and it appears that the copy or draft is identical in terms with the original, probate may be granted of that copy or draft, limited until the original is admitted to probate; or

   (b) if no such copy or draft is produced, probate may be granted of the contents of the will, if they can be sufficiently established, limited as above described.

Where will destroyed, etc.

Destroyed will

10. Where a will has been destroyed, otherwise than by the act or with the consent of the testator, probate may be granted of a copy or draft thereof, or of the contents thereof, if they can be sufficiently established.

Where will proved and deposited outside Singapore

Administration with copy annexed of authenticated copy of will proved abroad

11. When a will has been proved and deposited in a court of competent jurisdiction situated beyond the limits of Singapore, and a properly authenticated copy of the will is produced, probate may be granted of such copy or letters of administration may be granted with a copy of such copy annexed.

Where codicil propounded after probate

Codicil propounded after probate

12.—(1) Where, after probate has been granted, a codicil of the will is propounded, separate probate may be granted of the codicil.

(2) Where the codicil expressly or impliedly revokes the appointment of any executor to whom probate has been granted, the probate shall be revoked, and a new probate shall be granted of the will and codicil together.

Letters of administration with will annexed

On failure of executors

13.—(1) Where —

(a) no executor is appointed by a will;

(b) the executor or all the executors appointed by will are legally incapable of acting as such, or have renounced the right to act as such;

(c) no executor survives the testator;

(d) all the executors die before obtaining probate or before having administered all the estate of the deceased; or

(e) the executors appointed by any will do not appear and extract probate,

letters of administration with the will annexed may be granted to such person or persons as the court considers the fittest to administer the estate.

(2) A prior right to a grant under subsection (1) shall belong to the following persons in the following order:

(a) a universal or residuary legatee;

(b) a legal personal representative of a deceased universal or residuary legatee;

(c) such person or persons, being beneficiaries under the will, as would have been entitled to a grant of letters of administration if the deceased had died intestate;

(d) a legatee having a beneficial interest;

(e) a creditor of the deceased.

Letters of administration with will annexed may be granted to attorney of absent executor

14. Where an executor appointed by a will is absent from Singapore, and there is no other executor within Singapore willing to act, letters of administration with the will annexed may be granted to a duly authorised attorney of the absent executor, limited until he obtains probate for himself, and in the meantime to any purpose to which the attorney's authority is limited.

Grant to attorney of absent person entitled to letters of administration

15. Where any person to whom letters of administration with the will annexed might be granted under section 13 is absent from Singapore, letters of administration with the will annexed may be granted to his duly authorised attorney, limited as described in section 14.

Codicil propounded after grant of letters of administration

16. Section 12 shall apply in the case of a grant of letters of administration with the will annexed, in like manner as they apply in the case of a grant of probate.

Letters of administration until will produced

Letters of administration until will produced

17. When no will of the deceased is forthcoming, but there is reason to believe that there is a will in existence, letters of administration may be granted, limited until the will or an authenticated copy thereof is produced.

Letters of administration on intestacy

Letters of administration on intestacy

18.—(1) When a person has died intestate, the court may grant letters of administration of his estate.

(2) In granting such letters of administration the court shall have regard to the rights of all persons interested in the estate of the deceased person or the proceeds of sale thereof, and in regard to land settled previously to the death of the deceased, letters of administration may be granted to the trustees of the settlement.

(3) Any such grant of letters of administration may be limited in any wa the court thinks fit.

(4) Without prejudice to the generality of subsection (2) —

  (a) letters of administration may be granted to the husband or widow or next of kin or any of them;

  (b) when such persons apply for letters of administration, it shall be in the discretion of the court to grant them to any one or more of such persons;

(c) when no such person applies, letters of administration may be granted to a creditor of the deceased;

(d) in any case where —

    (i) the next of kin of any person dying intestate, or the greater number of such next of kin, so desire; or

    (ii) no next of kin or creditor or other person appears and makes out a claim to letters of administration,

letters of administration of the estate and effects of the intestate may be granted by the court to such person as the court thinks fit for the purpose.

(5) Nothing in this section shall affect any law by which special provision is made regarding the estates of persons of a particular religion or race.

Letters of administration pending probate action

Letters of administration pending probate action

20. Pending any probate action, letters of administration may be granted to such person as the court may appoint, limited so that the administrator shall not be empowered to distribute the estate, and shall be subject to such control by, and direction of, the court as the court thinks fit.

Letters of administration during infancy

Infants

21.—(1) No probate or letters of administration shall be granted to a person while he is an infant.

(2) Where an infant would, but for his infancy, be entitled to probate or letters of administration, letters of administration with or without the will annexed may, subject to section 6(1), be granted to the guardian of the person and property of the infant, or to such person as the court thinks fit, limited until the infant obtains a grant to himself.

(3) Where there are 2 or more infant executors or persons so entitled, any grant made under subsection (2) shall be limited until any of them obtains a grant.

Letters of administration during lunacy

Lunatics

22.—(1) No probate or letters of administration shall be granted to a lunatic or mentally disordered person.

[21/2008 wef 01/03/2010]

(2) Where any such person, if he is not mentally disordered, would be entitled to probate or letters of administration, letters of administration with or without the will annexed may be granted to the person to whom the care of his estate has been lawfully committed, or to such person as the court thinks fit, for the use and benefit of the lunatic or mentally disordered person, until he ceases to be mentally disordered and obtains a grant to himself.

[21/2008 wef 01/03/2010]

Letters of administration limited to trust property

Letters of administration of trust property

23. Where a person dies, leaving property in which he had no beneficial interest on his own account, and does not leave a representative who is able and willing to act, letters of administration, limited to such property, may be granted to the person beneficially interested in the property, or to some other person on his behalf.

Letters of administration limited to collection and preservation of property

Letters of administration to collect and preserve property

24. In any case in which it appears necessary for preserving the property of a deceased person, the court may grant to any person whom the court thinks fit letters of administration limited to the collection and preservation of the property of the deceased, and giving discharges of debts due to his estate, subject to the directions of the court.

Death of one of several executors, etc.

Death of one of several executors, etc.

25.—(1) Where probate or letters of administration have been granted to more than one executor or administrator, and one of them dies, the representation of the estate shall accrue to the surviving executor or executors or, except in cases to which section 6 applies, administrator or administrators.

(2) On the death of an administrator, letters of administration may be granted in respect of any estate not fully administered and in granting such letters of administration the court shall be guided by the same rules as apply to original grants.

Grants with exception

26.—(1) A grant of probate or letters of administration may be made subject to such exception as the will or the circumstances of the case require.

(2) A further grant may be made of the part of the estate excepted under subsection (1).

Administration when limited grant expired and some part of estate unadministered

27. When a limited grant has expired by effluxion of time or the happening of the event or contingency on which it was limited, and there is still some part of the deceased's estate unadministered, letters of administration shall be granted to those persons to whom original grants might have been made.

PART IV

OATH

Oath

28.—(1) Upon the grant of any probate or letters of administration, the grantee shall take an oath in the prescribed form, faithfully to administer the estate and to account for the same.

(2) Subsection (1) shall not apply where the grantee is the Public Trustee or a trust company.

[6/2004 wef 08/03/2004]

PART V

SECURITY

Administration bond

29.—(1) Where security is required the registrar shall determine its sufficiency.

(2) The security shall ordinarily be by bond in the prescribed form by the grantee and 2 sureties in the amount at which the estate within the jurisdiction is sworn, without deduction of any debts due by the deceased, other than debts secured by mortgage.

(3) The court or the registrar may for any sufficient reason increase or decrease the number of the sureties, or dispense with them, or reduce the amount of the bond.

[Act 27 of 2014 wef 01/01/2015]

(4) Where the Public Trustee has obtained a grant of letters of administration, he shall not be required to give security.

[6/2004 wef 08/03/2004]

(5) When the administrator is entitled to the whole of the estate after payment of the debts, sureties in the bond may ordinarily be dispensed with.

(6) Sureties may be required by the registrar to justify.

(7) Subject to subsection (8), in the case of administrations whether with or without the will annexed the person to whom the grant is made or on whose behalf it is sealed shall give security for the due administration of the estate.

[Act 27 of 2014 wef 01/01/2015]

(8) A grantee of letters of administration from a Family Court shall not be required to give security for the due administration of the estate unless —

   (a) the person for whose use and benefit the grant is made is an infant; or
   (b) the Family Court thinks fit to require such security.

[Act 27 of 2014 wef 01/01/2015]

PART VI

REVOCATION OF GRANT

Revocation of grant

32. Any probate or letters of administration may be revoked or amended for any sufficient cause.

PART IX

PROTECTION OF ESTATES PENDING GRANT

Vesting of estate in Public Trustee in certain circumstances between death and grant of administration

37.—(1) Where a person dies intestate, his real and personal estate shall vest in the Public Trustee.

[7/97]

(2) Where a testator dies and —

(a) at the time of his death there is no executor with power to obtain probate of the will; or

(b) at any time before probate of the will is granted there ceases to be any executor with power to obtain probate,

the real and personal estate of which the testator disposes by the will shall vest in the Public Trustee with effect from the time specified in paragraph (a) or (b) in relation to each case.

[7/97]

(3) The vesting by virtue of this section of any estate in the Public Trustee shall not, without more, confer or impose on him any power, duty, right, equity, obligation or liability in respect of the estate.

[7/97]

(4) Any estate or part of an estate vested in the Public Trustee under subsection (1) or (2) shall cease to be so vested on the grant of administration in respect of the estate or part in question.

[7/97]

PART X

RE-SEALING OF PROBATES AND LETTERS OF ADMINISTRATION GRANTED OUT OF SINGAPORE

Interpretation

46. In this Part —

"Commonwealth" shall, for the purposes of this Part, be deemed to include any country in the Commonwealth which the Minister may, by notification in the Gazette, specify to be a country to which this Part applies;

"court of probate" means any court or authority by whatever name designated, having jurisdiction in matters of probate;

"probate" and "letters of administration" include confirmation in Scotland and any instrument having in any country or territory the same effect which, under the law of Singapore, is given to probate or letters of administration respectively.

[45

[7/97; 2/99]

Power of court to re-seal

47.—(1) Subject to subsections (3) and (4), where —

  (a) a court of probate in any part of the Commonwealth has, either before, on or after 25th February 1999, granted probate or letters of administration in respect of the estate of a deceased person; or

  (b) a court of probate in a country or territory, being a country or territory declared by the Minister under subsection (5) as a country or territory to which this subsection applies, has, on or after a date specified by the Minister in respect of that country or territory (referred to in this section as the relevant date), granted probate or letters of administration in respect of the estate of a deceased person,

the probate or letters of administration so granted, or a certified copy thereof, sealed with the seal of the court granting the same, may, on being produced to and a copy thereof deposited in the High Court, be sealed with the seal of the Family Justice Courts.

[2/99]

[Act 27 of 2014 wef 01/01/2015]

(2) Upon sealing under subsection (1), the probate or letters of administration shall be of the like force and effect, and have the same operation in Singapore, as if granted by the High Court to the person by whom or on whose behalf the application for sealing was made.

[2/99]

(3) Before the probate or letters of administration is sealed with the seal of the Family Justice Courts, the High Court may require such evidence as it thinks fit as to the domicile of the deceased person.

[2/99]

[Act 27 of 2014 wef 01/01/2015]

(4) If it appears that the deceased was not, at the time of his death, domiciled within the jurisdiction of the court from which the grant was issued, the seal shall not be affixed unless the grant is such as the High Court would have made.

[2/99]

(5) For the purposes of subsection (1)(b), the Minister may, by notification in the Gazette —

  (a) declare any country or territory, which is not a part of the Commonwealth, as a country or territory to which subsection (1) applies; and

  (b) specify the relevant date in respect of that country or territory which may be a date before, on or after 25th February 1999.

[46

[2/99]

Provisions for estate duty

48. The provisions of the Estate Duty Act (Cap. 96), including the penal provisions thereof, shall apply as if the person who applies for sealing under this Part were an executor within the meaning of that Act, and section 42 of that Act shall apply with the necessary modifications to the re-sealing of grants under this Part.

Security on re-sealing letters of administration

49.—(1) Before the sealing of letters of administration under this Part, the administrator or his attorney shall give security by a bond in the prescribed form for the due administration of the estate.

(2) Such security shall be subject to section 29 relating to security to be given in the case of a grant of letters of administration.

Security for creditors in Singapore

50.—(1) Where the deceased has carried on business or resided in Singapore within 12 months of his death, the court may, on the application of a creditor of the deceased or otherwise, before a grant of probate or letters of administration is re-sealed, require adequate security to be given for the payment of debts due to creditors residing in Singapore.

[Act 27 of 2014 wef 01/01/2015]

(2) Any such creditor may give notice in writing to the registrar, requiring that he be notified of any application for the sealing of a grant of probate under this Part; and no such grant shall be sealed before the expiration of 7 days after service on such creditor of a notice in writing of an application for sealing.

Notice of sealing

51. Notice of the sealing of a grant under this Part shall be sent forthwith by the registrar to the court from which the grant is issued.

Notice of revocation

52. When notice has been received by the court of the re-sealing of a grant issued in Singapore, notice of any revocation or alteration of the grant shall be sent forthwith by the registrar to the court so re-sealing the grant.

53. [Repealed by Act 27 of 2014 wef 01/01/2015]

PART XI

GENERAL

Order to bring in will, etc.

54. The court may, on the application of any person interested, if it appears that there is reason to believe that any will or other testamentary document of a deceased person is in the possession or under the control of any person, or that any person has knowledge of

the existence of such a will or document, order that that person do, within a time named, produce the will or document at the registry, or attend at a time named before a court, for the purpose of being examined in relation to the will or document.

[Act 27 of 2014 wef 01/01/2015]

Grant to Public Trustee in cases of delay

55.—(1) In the following cases:

  (a) where, after the expiration of 6 months from the death of a deceased person, no application has been made for probate or letters of administration to his estate;

  (b) where any such application, though made within the said 6 months, has not within that period been proceeded with, or has been withdrawn or refused;

  (c) where any person, who has received a grant of letters of administration with or without the will annexed, neglects within one month of the date of the grant to give such security as he is lawfully required to furnish;

  (d) where a receiver may be appointed under section 39, but it appears that such appointment would not be a sufficient protection for the estate;

  (e) where an administrator has failed to extract the grant of letters of administration; or

  (f) where after the death of a last surviving executor or administrator of a deceased person's estate 6 months have elapsed and no application for the representation of the estate has been made,

letters of administration with or without the will annexed may be granted to the Public Trustee, or to such other person as the court thinks fit.

[6/2004 wef 08/03/2004]

(2) Nothing in this section shall be construed so as to prevent the Public Trustee from applying for or being granted letters of administration of the estate of a deceased person with or without the will annexed before the expiration of a period of 6 months of the death of the deceased.

[6/2004 wef 08/03/2004]

Death of payee

56.—(1) When funds in court are by an order directed to be paid, transferred or delivered to any person named or described in an order, or in a certificate of the registrar, except to a person therein expressed to be entitled to those funds as trustee, executor, or administrator, or otherwise than in his own right, or for his own use, the funds, or any portion thereof for the time being remaining unpaid, untransferred or undelivered, may, unless the order otherwise directs, on proof of the death of such person, whether on or after or, in the case of payment directed to be made to a creditor as such, before the date of the order, be paid, transferred, or delivered to the legal personal representatives of the deceased person, or to the survivors or survivor of them.

(2) If no administration has been taken out to the estate of such deceased person who has died intestate, and whose assets do not exceed $500, including the amount of the funds directed to be so paid, transferred or delivered to him, the funds may be paid, transferred or delivered to the person who, being a widower, widow, child, father, mother, brother or sister of the deceased, would be entitled to take administration to his or her estate upon a declaration by that person in the prescribed form.

Administration of assets

57.—(1) Where the estate of a deceased person is insolvent his estate shall be administered in accordance with the rules set out in the First Schedule.

(2) The right of retainer of a personal representative and his right to prefer creditors may be exercised in respect of all assets of the deceased, but the right of retainer shall only apply to debts owing to the personal representative in his own right whether solely or jointly with another person.

(3) Subject to subsection (2), nothing in this Act shall affect the right of retainer of a personal representative, or his right to prefer creditors.

(4) Where the estate of a deceased person is solvent his estate shall, subject to the Rules of Court (Cap. 322, R 5) and section 58 as to charges on property of the deceased, and to the provisions, if any, contained in his will, be applicable towards the discharge of the funeral, testamentary and administration expenses, debts and liabilities payable thereout in the order mentioned in the Second Schedule.

Charges on property of deceased to be paid primarily out of property charged

58.—(1) Where a person dies possessed of, or entitled to, or, under a general power of appointment, by his will disposes of an interest in property which at the time of his death is charged with the payment of money, whether by way of legal mortgage, equitable charge or otherwise (including lien for unpaid purchase money), and the deceased has not by will, deed or other document signified a contrary or other intention, the interest so charged shall, as between the different persons claiming through the deceased, be primarily liable for the payment of the charge.

(2) Every part of the interest referred to on subsection (1), according to its value, shall bear a proportionate part of the charge on the whole thereof.

(3) Such contrary or other intention shall not be deemed to be sigified —

   (a) by a general direction for the payment of debts or of the debts of the testator out of his movable property or of his residuary estate; or

   (b) by a charge of debts upon any such estate,

unless such intention is further signified by words expressly or by necessary implication referring to all or some part of the charge.

(4) Nothing in this section shall affect the right of a person entitled to the charge to obtain payment or satisfaction thereof either out of the other assets of the deceased or otherwise.

Administration by Public Trustee

62.—(1) Where any person dies leaving property in Singapore not exceeding $50,000 in value (without deduction for debts), the Public Trustee, after satisfying himself that no application for letters of administration is pending, may, if he thinks fit, by writing signed by him declare that he undertakes to administer such property.

[42/2005 wef 01/01/2006]

(1A) For the purpose of subsection (1), the amount of $50,000 shall not include —

   (a) the value of any property which the deceased possessed or was entitled to as trustee and not beneficially; and

(b) in the case of a person who dies on or after 17th September 2005, any moneys payable by an appointed insurer pursuant to the Dependants' Protection Insurance Scheme or any other equivalent scheme maintained by the Central Provident Fund Board under the Central Provident Fund Act (Cap. 36).

[42/2005 wef 01/01/2006]

(2) Upon a declaration under subsection (1), the Public Trustee shall be empowered to administer such property as though letters of administration, with or without the will annexed, of the estate of the deceased person had been granted to him, and his receipt shall be a sufficient discharge to any person who pays any money or delivers any property to him.

[6/2004 wef 08/03/2004]

(3) Notice of every declaration made under subsection (1) shall be given to the registrar.

[7/76]

[Act 16 of 2016 wef 10/06/2016]

(4) At any time prior to the distribution of any part of the property among the beneficiaries thereof under this section the Public Trustee may, if he thinks it expedient to do so, notwithstanding any declaration made by him under subsection (1), decline to proceed with the administration of the property in his hands until a grant of representation has been obtained in respect of the estate of the deceased.

[6/2004 wef 08/03/2004]

Payment for minor's maintenance, etc., out of property not exceeding $25,000 in value held by Public Trustee

63.—(1) Where any property not exceeding $25,000 in value is held by the Public Trustee, whether by virtue of a grant of letters of administration to him or by virtue of the powers conferred on him by this Act, and the property is held by him upon trust for any person for any interest whatsoever, whether vested or contingent, then, subject to any prior interest or charges affecting that property, the Public Trustee may in his sole discretion, during the minority of any such person, in respect of that person's maintenance, education or benefit make payments of the whole or such part of the income and capital money of such property as may in all the circumstances be reasonable.

[7/76]

[6/2004 wef 08/03/2004]

(2) When the property so held exceeds $25,000 but does not exceed $50,000 in value, the Public Trustee may make such payments of capital money to the extent of $25,000.

[7/76]

[6/2004 wef 08/03/2004]

(3) Such payments may be made to the parent or guardian of such person or otherwise as the Public Trustee may, in his discretion, determine, and whether or not there is —

(a) any other fund applicable to the same purpose; or

(b) any person bound by law to provide for such person's maintenance or education.

[6/2004 wef 08/03/2004]

Exemption from necessity of giving notice of distribution of property of less than $10,000 in value

64.—(1) Where the total value of any property (without deduction for debts, but not including the value of any property which the deceased possessed or was entitled to as trustee and not beneficially) administered by the Public Trustee, whether by virtue of a grant of letters of administration to him or by virtue of the powers conferred on him by this Act, does not exceed $10,000, it shall not be necessary for the Public Trustee to give notice by advertisement in the Gazette or otherwise of his intention to distribute the estate or require any person interested to send in particulars of his claim against the estate, but the Public Trustee may proceed forthwith to convey or distribute the estate or any part thereof to or among the persons entitled thereto, having regard only to the claims, whether formal or not, of which the Public Trustee then had notice.

[6/2004 wef 08/03/2004]

(2) The Public Trustee shall not, as respects the property conveyed or distributed under subsection (1), be liable to any person of whose claim the Public Trustee has not had notice at the time of conveyance or distribution.

[6/2004 wef 08/03/2004]

(3) Nothing in this section shall —

    (a) prejudice the right of any person to follow the property representing the same, into the hands of any person, other than a purchaser, who may have received it; or

    (b) free the Public Trustee from any obligation to make searches similar to those which an intending purchaser would be advised to make or obtain.

[7/76]

[6/2004 wef 08/03/2004]

When interest is payable into Consolidated Fund

65.—(1) Where any trust money in the hands of the Public Trustee is normally insufficient to earn bank interest if kept in a bank current account the money may be kept in a general banking account or deposited in any bank.

[6/2004 wef 08/03/2004]

(2) Any interest allowed by the bank shall be paid into the Consolidated Fund.

Executors' or administrators' commission

66.—(1) The court may in its or his discretion allow the executors or administrators a commission not exceeding 5% on the value of the assets collected by them, but in the allowance or disallowance of such commission the court shall be guided by its or his approval or otherwise of their conduct in the administration of the estate.

[Act 27 of 2014 wef 01/01/2015]

(2) The registrar may, in the course of the taking of the administration accounts of executors or administrators, exercise the powers conferred on the court by subsection (1).

[Act 27 of 2014 wef 01/01/2015]

Testamentary and funeral expenses

67.—(1) The court shall allow the executors or administrators the reasonable testamentary and other expenses incurred by them, and also proper funeral expenses and all reasonable expenses of subsequent religious ceremonies suitable to the station in life of the deceased.

[Act 27 of 2014 wef 01/01/2015]

(2) The registrar may, in the course of the taking of the administration accounts of executors or administrators, exercise the powers conferred on the court by subsection (1).

[Act 27 of 2014 wef 01/01/2015]

Where funds of estate cannot be immediately distributed

68.—(1) Where, upon the conclusion of the administration of the estate of a person dying testate or intestate, there remain in the hands of the personal representative funds of which he is unable to dispose immediately by distribution in accordance with law by reason of the inability of the person entitled to give a discharge, through lack of legal capacity or otherwise, or for any other cause which to the Public Trustee appears sufficient, the personal representative may, if the Public Trustee consents to accept the same, pay those funds to the Public Trustee who —

(a) shall not be required to make any enquiry whether the administration has been conducted in accordance with law;

(b) may accept those funds as a trustee for the person entitled, and apply the same for the benefit of such person; and

(c) may for such purpose exercise all the powers conferred on him under section 63.

[6/2004 wef 08/03/2004]

(2) The receipt of the Public Trustee may be accepted by the personal representative and shall constitute a full and sufficient discharge in respect of such funds.

[6/2004 wef 08/03/2004]

Power of registrar to grant probate or letters of administration in uncontested cases

69. Notwithstanding anything to the contrary in this Act, the registrar may exercise and shall be deemed always to have had power to exercise, in uncontested matters and subject to rules made under any written law for the time being in force relating to the courts, all or any of the powers conferred upon the court by Parts II, III and X, and by section 55.

FIRST SCHEDULE

Section 57(1)

RULES AS TO PAYMENT OF DEBTS WHERE ESTATE IS INSOLVENT

1. The funeral, testamentary and administration expenses shall have priority.

2. Subject to paragraph 1, the same rules shall prevail and be observed as to the respective rights of secured and unsecured creditors and as to debts and liabilities provable and as to the valuation of annuities and future and contingent liabilities respectively, and as to the priorities of debts and liabilities, as may be in force for the time being under the law of bankruptcy with respect to the assets of persons adjudged bankrupt.

SECOND SCHEDULE

Section 57(4)

ORDER OF APPLICATION OF ASSETS WHERE THE ESTATE IS SOLVENT

1. Property of the deceased undisposed of by will, subject to the retention thereout of a fund sufficient to meet any pecuniary legacies.

2. Property of the deceased not specifically devised or bequeathed but included (either by a specific or general description) in a residuary gift, subject to the retention out of such property of a fund sufficient to meet any pecuniary legacies, so far as not provided for as aforesaid.

3. Property of the deceased specifically appropriated or devised or bequeathed (either by a specific or general description) for the payment of debts.

4. Property of the deceased charged with, or devised or bequeathed (either by a specific or general description) subject to a charge for the payment of debts.

5. The fund, if any, retained to meet pecuniary legacies.

6. Property specifically devised or bequeathed, rateably according to value.

7. Property appointed by will under a general power, rateably according to value.

8. The following provisions shall also apply:

(a) the order of application may be varied by the will of the deceased; and

(b) this Schedule does not affect the liability of land to answer the death duty imposed thereon in exoneration of other assets.

LEGITIMACY ACT
(CHAPTER 162)
(Original Enactment: Ordinance 20 of 1934)
REVISED EDITION 1985
(30th March 1987)

An Act to provide for the legitimation of children born out of wedlock.

[18th May 1934]

Short title

1. This Act may be cited as the Legitimacy Act.

Interpretation

2. In this Act, unless there is something repugnant in the subject or context —

"court" means the High Court or a Family Court;

[Act 27 of 2014 wef 01/10/2014]

"date of legitimation" means the date of the marriage leading to the legitimation, or, where the marriage occurred before 18th May 1934, that day;

"disposition" means an assurance of any interest in property by any instrument whether inter vivos or by will;

"intestate" includes a person who leaves a will but dies intestate as to some beneficial interest in his estate;

"legitimated person" means a person legitimated by this Act;

"will" includes "codicil".

Legitimation by subsequent marriage of parents

3.—(1) Subject to this section, where the parents of an illegitimate person marry or have married one another, whether before, on or after 18th May 1934 the marriage shall, if the father or mother of the illegitimate person was or is at the date of the marriage domiciled in Singapore, render that person, if living, legitimate from 18th May 1934 or from the date of the marriage, whichever last happens.

[Act 16 of 2013 wef 01/10/2014]

(2) Nothing in this Act shall operate to legitimate a person unless the marriage leading to the legitimation was solemnized and registered in accordance with the provisions of the repealed Christian Marriage Ordinance [Cap. 37, 1955 Ed.] or of the Civil Marriage Ordinance [Cap. 38, 1955 Ed.] or unless that marriage was registered or deemed to be registered under the Women's Charter [Cap. 353].

(3) The legitimation of a person under this Act does not enable him or his spouse, children or remoter issue to take any interest in property save as hereinafter expressly provided in this Act.

(4) The provisions contained in the Schedule shall have effect with respect of the re-registration of the births of legitimated persons.

Declarations of legitimacy of legitimated persons

4.—(1) A person claiming that he or his parent or any remoter ancestor became or has become a legitimated person may, whether domiciled in Singapore or elsewhere, and whether a citizen of Singapore or not, apply to the court by originating summons for a decree declaring that the applicant is the legitimate child of his parents, or that his parent or remoter ancestor was legitimate, and the court shall have jurisdiction to hear and determine that application and to make such decree declaratory of the legitimacy or illegitimacy of such person as to the court may seem just; and that decree shall be binding to all intents and purposes on the Government and on all persons whomsoever.

[42/2005 wef 01/01/2006]

[Act 27 of 2014 wef 01/10/2014]

(2) Every application under this section shall be supported by an affidavit verifying the facts alleged in the same, and by such proof of the absence of fraud and collusion, as the court may by any general rule direct.

[42/2005 wef 01/01/2006]

(3) In all proceedings under this section the court shall have full power to award and enforce payment of costs to any person cited, whether that person does or does not oppose the declaration applied

for, in case the court considers it reasonable that the costs should be paid.

(4) A copy of every application under this section and of the affidavit in support thereof shall be served on the Attorney-General, who may apply to intervene in the application if he thinks necessary.

[42/2005 wef 01/01/2006]

(5) Where any application is made under this section to the court, the person or persons, if any, besides the Attorney-General as the court thinks fit shall, subject to the rules made under this section, be cited to the proceedings or otherwise summoned in such manner as the court directs, and may be permitted to become parties to the proceedings, and oppose the application.

(6) The decree of the court shall not in any case prejudice any person —

  (a) if it is subsequently proved to have been obtained by fraud or collusion; or

  (b) unless that person has been cited or made a party to the proceedings or is the heir at law, next of kin, or other real or personal representative of, or derives title under or through, a person so cited or made a party.

(7) No proceedings to be had under this section shall affect any final judgment or decree already pronounced or made by any court of competent jurisdiction.

(8) The Family Justice Rules Committee constituted under section 46(1) of the Family Justice Act 2014 may make Family Justice Rules for carrying the provisions of this section into effect.

[Act 27 of 2014 wef 01/01/2015]

(9) The Family Justice Rules may, instead of providing for any matter, refer to any provision made or to be made about that matter by practice directions issued for the time being by the registrar of the Family Justice Courts.

[Act 27 of 2014 wef 01/01/2015]

Rights of legitimated persons to take interests in property

5.—(1) Subject to the provisions of this Act a legitimated person and his spouse, children or remoter issue shall be entitled to take any interest —

(a) in the estate of an intestate dying after the date of legitimation;

(b) under any disposition coming into operation after the date of legitimation,

in the like manner as if the legitimated person had been born legitimate.

(2) Where the right to any property depends on the relative seniority of the children of any person, and those children include one or more legitimated persons, the legitimated person or persons shall rank as if he or they had been born on the day when he or they became legitimated by virtue of this Act, and if more than one such legitimated person became legitimated at the same time they shall rank as between themselves in order of seniority.

(3) This section applies only if and so far as a contrary intention is not expressed in the disposition, and shall have effect subject to the terms of the disposition and to the provisions therein contained.

Succession on intestacy of legitimated persons and their issue

6. Where a legitimated person or a child or remoter issue of a legitimated person dies intestate in respect of any of his property, the same persons shall be entitled to take the same interests therein as they would have been entitled to take if the legitimated person had been legitimate.

Application to illegitimate person dying before marriage of parents

7. Where an illegitimate person dies on or after 18th May 1934 and before the marriage of his parents leaving any spouse, children or remoter issue living at the date of the marriage, then if that person would, if living at the time of the marriage of his parents, have become a legitimated person, the provisions of this Act with respect to the taking of interests in property by, or in succession to, the spouse, children and remoter issue of a legitimated person shall apply as if that person had been a legitimated person and the date of the marriage of his parents had been the date of legitimation.

Personal rights and obligations of legitimated persons

8. A legitimated person shall have the same rights and be under the same obligations in respect of the maintenance and support of himself or of any other person as if he had been born legitimate, and, subject to the provisions of this Act, the provisions of any Act relating to

claims for damages, compensation, allowance, benefit, or otherwise by or in respect of a legitimate child shall apply in the like manner in the case of a legitimated person.

Provisions as to legitimation by extraneous law

9.—(1) Where the parents of an illegitimate person marry or have married one another, whether before, on or after 18th May 1934 and the father of the illegitimate person was or is, at the time of the marriage, domiciled in a country other than Singapore, by the law of which the illegitimate person became legitimated by virtue of the subsequent marriage, that person, if living, shall within Singapore be recognised as having been so legitimated from 17th May 1934 or from the date of the marriage, whichever last happens, notwithstanding that his father was not at the time of the birth of that person domiciled in a country in which legitimation by subsequent marriage was permitted by law.

(2) All the provisions of this Act relating to legitimated persons and to the taking of interests in property by or in succession to a legitimated person and the spouse, children and remoter issue of a legitimated person shall apply in the case of a person recognised as having been legitimated under this section, or who would, had he survived the marriage of his parents, have been so recognised; and accordingly this Act shall have effect as if references therein to a legitimated person included a person so recognised as having been legitimated.

(3) For the purposes of this section, "country" includes any part of the British Commonwealth, as well as a foreign country.

Right of illegitimate child and mother of illegitimate child to succeed on intestacy of the other

10.—(1) Where, on or after 18th May 1934, the mother of an illegitimate child, the child not being a legitimated person, dies intestate as respects all or any of her property, and does not leave any legitimate issue her surviving, the illegitimate child, or if he is dead his issue, shall be entitled to take any interest therein to which he or his issue would have been entitled if he had been born legitimate.

(2) Where, on or after 18th May 1934, an illegitimate child, not being a legitimated person, dies intestate as respects all or any of his property, his mother, if surviving, shall be entitled to take any interest therein to which she would have been entitled if the child had been born legitimate and she had been the only surviving parent.

Saving

11. Nothing in this Act shall affect the operation or construction of any disposition coming into operation before 18th May 1934 or affect any rights under the intestacy of a person dying before that date.

THE SCHEDULE

Section 3(4)

REGISTRATION OF BIRTHS OF LEGITIMATED PERSONS

1. The Registrar-General of Births and Deaths may, on production of such evidence as appears to him to be satisfactory, authorise at any time the re-registration of the birth of a legitimated person whose birth is already registered under the Registration of Births and Deaths Act [Cap. 267], and the re-registration shall be effected in such manner and at such place as the Registrar-General may by regulations prescribe:

Provided that the Registrar-General shall not authorise the re-registration of the birth of any such person in any case where information with a view to obtaining such re-registration is not furnished to him by both parents unless —

(a) the paternity of the legitimated person has been established by an affiliation order or otherwise by a decree of a court of competent jurisdiction; or

(b) a declaration of the legitimacy of the legitimated person has been made by the court under section 4.

[Act 27 of 2014 wef 01/10/2014]

2. It shall be the duty of the parents of a legitimated person, or, in cases where re-registration can be effected on information furnished by one parent and one of the parents is dead, of the surviving parent, within 3 months after the date of the marriage, to furnish to the Registrar-General information with a view to obtaining the re-registration of the birth of that person.

3. Where the parents, or either of them, fail to furnish the necessary information within the time limited for the purpose, the Registrar-General may at any time after the expiration of that time require the parents of a person whom he believes to have been legitimated by virtue of this Act, or either of them, to give him such information concerning the matter as he may consider necessary, verified in such

manner as he may direct, and for that purpose to attend personally either at his office or at any other place appointed by him within such time, not being less than 7 days after the receipt of the notice, as may be specified in the notice.

4. The failure of the parents or either of them to furnish information as required by this Schedule in respect of any legitimated person shall not affect the legitimation of that person.

5. No fee for re-registration under this Schedule shall be charged if the necessary information for the purpose is furnished within the time above specified; but in any other case there shall be charged in respect of the re-registration such fees, not exceeding in the aggregate $2, as may be prescribed by regulations made under this Schedule.

6. This Schedule shall be construed as one with the Registration of Births and Deaths Act.

ABOUT THE AUTHOR

Lim Fung Peen is a director of Yuen Law LLC and a veteran of the legal industry, having been in practice since 1997. He started out in general and commercial litigation and transitioned to focus more on family, inheritance and matrimonial work at the request of his clients. He currently heads the firm's Family and Private Wealth team and helps his clients in matters such as Mental Capacity Act deputyship, adoption, bankruptcy, property and conveyancing, divorce, employment, Wills, Lasting Power of Attorney, trusts and probate, estate planning, power of attorney, deed of family arrangements, tax, contentious family/matrimonial matters, employment/HR issues and more. His clients have included government statutory boards and well-known MNCs and SMEs, as well as expatriates and foreigners.

His team was ranked in *The Straits Times*' "Singapore Best Law Firms 2021" in the Family as well as Inheritance and Succession Private Wealth Management categories.

As a family man, Fung Peen strives to learn more about how to be a better husband and father, and this has in turn spurred him to help other families where he can. He considers it a great privilege and blessing to be able to help others by providing practical legal advice to resolve their family issues.